DIVINE FOOTSTEPS

JOURNEYING THROUGH
TIME WITH GOD

Dr. Aretha Coleman-Terry

DIVINE FOOTSTEPS: Journeying Through Time with God

Copyright © 2024 by Dr. Aretha Coleman-Terry

Book and Cover design by Pamela D. Cox
ISBN : 978-1-7372225-3-8 (Print)
First Edition

Scriptures are taken from the KING JAMES VERSION (KJV): KING JAMES VERSION, public domain, unless otherwise noted.

THERE IS...

An Appointed Time

A Set Time

A Waiting Time

But it Will Happen in God's Time!

Table of Contents

DEDICATION   6

PREFACE   8

CHAPTER ONE

Indifferent Times but I Still Trusted God.................. 10

CHAPTER TWO

Bad Times Are in God's Hands............................26

CHAPTER THREE

My Times Are in God's Hands.............................34

CHAPTER FOUR

God is No Respecter of Persons...........................38

CHAPTER FIVE

I Didn't Understand God's Timing.......................42

CHAPTER SIX

The Omnipotent...50

CHAPTER SEVEN

Omniscient 54

CHAPTER EIGHT

Omnipresent 60

CHAPTER NINE

Stop Worrying and Start Trusting God....................68

CHAPTER TEN

God Told Me, "I AM THINE." 78

CHAPTER ELEVEN

Heed to God's Calling and Warning......................86

CHAPTER TWELVE

Repentance...Forgiveness...Obedience................114

CHAPTER THIRTEEN

But When the Fullness of Time Has Come...God's
Appointed Time and the Set Time. 118

CHAPTER FOURTEEN

But When the Fullness of Time Had Come for Me...
the Appointed Time and the Set Time 132

CHAPTER FIFTEEN

This Appointed Time Led Me to Great Finances144

CHAPTER SIXTEEN

God's Preparation to My Appointed Time of
Victories... 154

About the Author..156

DEDICATION

This book is dedicated to my grandmother, Rosie Lee Mott, my parents, George and Rosie Lee Coleman, and my sibling Regina, who have all gone on before me.

MY INTERCESSORS
Pastor Don Coleman
Pastor Elizabeth Humes
Dr. Debra Graham
Evangelist Tina Smith

MY CHEERLEADERS
Evangelist Verda Bowers
Lady Joanne Boyland
DeBorah Jennings

MY FAMILY
Pastor Calvin and Evangelist Shirley Coleman
Elder Silesia Franklin and Deacon Willie Franklin
Brother Danny and the late Marlise Coleman

MY BELOVED GODCHILDREN SENT FROM GOD
Trina Bohanner
Charles Durrett
Julius Williams
Keith Turks
Aretha Lae Yarbrough
Stephen and Tricia Pollion

MY GODSENDS
Pamela D. Cox
Veronica Holmes

PREFACE

As you read this book and peruse the testimonies, you will know that God determines how long we wait in "His Waiting Room." One thing I can assure you is that waiting time is not wasted time with God. God appoints the times in our lives. God told me, "He Is Time." Sometimes the times in His waiting room can be the same day, overnight, a week, a month, a year, or many, many years. It is in God's timing that some will never make it out of the waiting room. *"And these all having obtained a good report through faith, received not the promise" (Hebrews 11:39).* That was God's appointed time for them. Every human being upon the face of the earth has an appointment with God. Our times are in His hands, and our lives. They are His appointed times according to His appointed means to bring about His appointed ends. God's appointed time has a set date and time when His divine timing will come forth.

Solomon, the author of Ecclesiastes in the Bible, says there are appointed times for specific events to occur in our lives that are totally out of our control because God has the key to timing. God has sovereignly set the times, including appointing the times for our trials as well as our blessings. His timing is always

8

good, right, and appropriate. "It is up to us to use our faith in Him to remain in a good attitude, to enjoy the moments," says Dr. Nadolyn Dunigan. This is the time He has set for us to grow, overcome, and meet the responsibilities or trials imposed. Every day from the moment we wake up until we go back to sleep, we are watching the time, setting time, meeting schedules, or calculating how much time we have. This highlights that everything matters because we have only so much time. God schedules and performs everything at exactly the right time. The sovereign God can exercise control of all things in our lives, not just "time."

CHAPTER ONE
Indifferent Times but I Still Trusted God

When I was in elementary school, I wanted to participate in everything the school had to offer. I wanted to go on field trips to the zoo, Ringling Bros. and Barnum & Bailey Circus, museums, and plays, and I really wanted my "School Day" pictures taken. I even desired to attend the sock hops, which are now called "School Dances." I was born with an outgoing personality, so all these activities actuated my appetite for school fulfillment. Out of the entire six years in elementary school, I was blessed to take one school day picture, and that was that on that! Nevertheless, I did survive. I was not sad, disheartened, or taunted by peer pressure. I had the mindset that my parents knew what was best for me. I did not realize or learn until later in life that my parents were not financially able to accommodate those activities, with one income supporting a household of six children. During the "kinder and gentler" days, we did not question our parents, or even say, "How come?" When our parents said no, no was no. When they said yes, yes was yes. There was no in-between, and you didn't go ask the other parent. Nor could we say, "Everybody else is going" or "Everybody else is doing it." We said yes ma'am and went on and lived on. Job 14:14b says, *"All the Days of My Appointed Time, Will I Wait, Till My Change come."*

My career led me to become a teacher, which gave me the opportunity to take my students on field trips to the circus, museums, and plays. I was finally able to have my School Day pictures taken every year for free because I was a teacher and often the sponsor of those events. All the teacher's pictures would be in the front of every yearbook. Those things I desired as a child, had a set time to come to fruition. God did not give me the desires of my heart during my childhood, but He knew I would have the opportunities later in life as a teacher, unbeknownst to me. Paul said, *"But when the fullness of the time was come" (Galatians 4:4a)*. God had a set time and an appointed time for me to experience and take part in each event. God has an auspicious time and momentous time for our life. "The fullness of time" underscores God's incursion into time with His answer for people.

During my high school years, I attended three different schools due to a house fire, my parents moving to a nice neighborhood and owning their first home, and school redistricting. Many of the students at the second jr. high school I attended were very affluent. They came from a two-parent dwelling, and lived in big, beautiful suburbia-type homes. Their clothes were fashionable, and they had several changes of shoes to match their outfits. Their hair was always fixed and had nice gold pendants and jewelry. They did not receive free lunches, they brought their lunches and had money to buy whatever they wanted in the cafeteria to add to their lunches. My parents never qualified for me to get a free lunch and I had no extra money to buy anything in the cafeteria but a carton of milk for three cents. Oh, how I wished I had two more cents to get a package of oatmeal cookies. Every now and then, far, and in between, the Lord would bless, or someone would give me a big oatmeal cookie. Cookies were very large back then. You would receive five cookies for a nickel and then they went down to four cookies for a nickel. I was so humbly happy to get just one.

Back then all students took pride in their grades. Everybody wanted an A or B. It was no big deal to me, for some unforeseen reason. I was just an average student. I didn't know how to study, but I knew to do my homework. Reviewing the day's lesson for reinforcement never crossed my mind, and my parents didn't push it either. As long as I was not bringing home D's and F's, I was doing fine in school to all that was concerned. I was just a happy average Jr. High student. Those more affluent students went on out-of-town trips with the school during our spring break. I already knew not to show the flyer or discuss the out-of-town trip with my parents. I am the same student whose parents were not financially able to let me go on in-town trips.

My parents had just purchased our first home and bought their first new car instead of a used one. By being brought up in the church, I was somehow happy and content. My mother would always pray with us in the home. Looking back now, not liking it then, it brought us much peace, unity, harmony, and respect for both of our parents. We were too young to understand the power of prayer. My brother and I remark, even now, how our parents gave us a wonderful life, laced with prayer, and took us to prayer meetings. We did not like it or appreciate it then, because we wanted to be like other children. As we began to be promoted to the next grade and on to the next grade, we saw our childhood friends and peers were getting into grown people things, such as cussing, drinking, smoking, drugs, and involved in sex. We knew then those students did not have the background we had, they did not have the fear of God in their lives, their parents were very liberal and saying and doing everything in front of them. We immediately saw that what our parents were doing was so meaningful and needful. We never faced peer pressure, nor did we desire those habits. We didn't sneak around to fit in or be accepted by the in-crowd either. We were taught to go the other way or leave the restroom immediately if we would walk up on things that were not lawful or child friendly. It was PRAYER, PRAYER, PRAYER! My parents prayed with us and kept us in church and church activities. Looking back, I realize that these experiences built our self-esteem, and we never experienced peer pressure. As I stated earlier, I was just an ordinary, average student academically. *"But when the fullness of time was come"* (Galatians 4:4a). God had a set time and an appointed time for me to experience and take part in each event. God has an auspicious time and momentous time for our lives. "The fullness of time" underscores God's incursion into time with His answer for people.

God blessed me to become the Spelling Bee Champion in the eighth grade of my school. The city newspaper spotlighted me with my picture. PRAYER, PRAYER! I became very, very popular, just from that at school. That is when my smile and personality started blossoming. That helped me all the way through college. We did not have computers and cell phones to use "spell check." I have always been known for speaking and spelling. Out of all the students in the school, my principal wanted me to come over to his home and drill his daughter with spelling words on Saturdays. I felt honored and well sought after among all the other well-dressed students who came from diverse backgrounds and were college-bound, already knowing what they wanted to be in life. When I was asked what I wanted to be, I simply said, "a secretary"—that was only as far as my ambition would lead me. I could not hardly wait to tell my mom the good news about me being the Spelling Bee Champion, and my principal wanted me to come over to his house every Saturday to help his daughter with her spelling words. No one ever helped me, neither was I drilled. It was just something God did through my mother's prayers with us. My mother immediately said, "NO!" empathically, and said, "We don't know nothing about that man or his wife." She said, "You have to be careful for nothing." What sounded like a good idea, was not a God idea. Now that I look back, I did see the lust in his eyes. I was just happy to be noticed and thought of so greatly by my principal. He knew I was a vulnerable, inexperienced, church girl. That is why parents should be concerned about their children, who they hang around, where they are going, and meet both parents of their friends or associates. Sometimes, you can learn a lot through a visit or a phone conversation.

Parents should carry their children to their events and go back to pick them up. Yes, I know children can get into things between their dropping off and picking up times. They still know you are involved and watching. There is only so much they can do. That's why parents need a prayer life with God, and their children should attend church weekly so that God can be there for them. If you take care of God's business, He will take care of your business and let you in on some things.

My mother had never seen or met with the principal at my school. God gave her the wisdom that it would not be a good thing, although most parents would love to have bragged and boasted on the invitation. My mother saw through the eyes of God the pitfalls that come with things that start out so innocently. I was fully developed to be an eighth-grade student. I was just right for the plucking in a lustful man's eyes. Even though I did not have a relationship with God, I was His property. He knew what I was to become. He knew He had plans for me that was good and not evil. He knew one day, I would be a teacher, public speaker, a minister, a philanthropist, and an author, just to mention a few of my God-given gifts.

The next year, I joined the Glee Club, which is now known as the Show Choir or Swing Choir. I did not have a lead voice, but I was great at backing and carrying out strong alto and tenor notes. My parents felt comfortable with me playing a part in this for the school. I was already singing in the junior choir at church and singing with a small segment of the junior choir members on the radio every Sunday. Coca Cola sponsored us. As I shared earlier, I was not one of the affluent students. My parents instilled righteousness in us at an early age. We grew up God-fearing, honoring our mother and father, and obeying those in authority over us.

Children always thought I was so proper. What they saw was that I was different from them because I had a calling upon my life. My parents instilled values, morals, etiquette, self-esteem, and self-worth in our lives, but it was the Word of God that my mother drilled into us daily until it became a

15

household word and name that sustained us. That is where all my successes, blessings, and favors came from. It was not my present condition, but my future potential in God. My outlook looked gloomy, but my uplook was glorious. We should never ever judge a book by its cover. We will never know when God will step in and work a miracle and bring things to existence. *"My times are in thy hand"* *(Psalm 31:15)*.

My high school years were approaching quickly. I still had no idea or inkling of what I wanted to be, but I knew I was going to matriculate into a college or university. That was not an option for me. It was understood that I was going to attend, but deciding on my major was something I had to figure out along the way while I was attending.

I joined the Drama Club and Glee Club again. I've always loved acting, speaking, and singing. Today, at 67 years old, I still enjoy all of these activities. The Drama Club helped me to get out of stage fright and visualize success. It sharpened my communication skills and how to tolerate people from all kinds of backgrounds. It really broadened my horizons. I am not afraid to ask for anything or tell people what I want and how I want it. It gave me boldness. I was not in the top ten percent of my graduating class of 502 students, but I was in the top twenty percentile. I was number 102 out of 502 students. I was not in the in-crowd or walked in on graduation evening with honor cords. *"But when the fullness of time was come"* *(Galatians 4:4a).* **God had a set time and appointed time for me to come forth.**

In our class superlatives, I received the most votes for "Miss Charm." My God given smile came into fruition in the eighth grade. God magnified my smile. I was the chaplain for the Student Government Association (SGA). I had no idea on graduation night, the SGA would be the ones to lead in the senior class. I thought it would be the Valedictorian and the Salutatorian that would lead the graduating class in. There I was number four in line out of fifty students leading the senior class in! It was the President, Vice President, Secretary, Chaplain, and Parliamentarian of the SGA that led our class in. God has a way of making a way for you. We were in front of the Valedictorian, Salutatorian, the Top Ten percent of the graduating class, the National Honor Society, and students with distinguished cords around their necks. We did not sit on the floor, we sat on the stage with the Sr. Advisor, Board of Education members, and the keynote speaker. I was the Chaplain, so I did the opening scripture in front of 12,000 people at the coliseum! Being a member of the Drama Club helped me overcome stage fright through reciting many speeches at church and participating in oratorical contests. I must credit God for His role in my journey. It was Him for the most part who gave me the resilience. I will never forget that night because they told us that we would march in according to your class rank, which mine was 102! But God! *"But when the fullness of time was come" (Galatians 4:4a). "My times are in your hands" (Psalm 31:15).*

God saw fit for me to be number four in marching in and sitting on stage with other dignitaries from the Board of Education. I will never forget that night and the scriptures that were selected for me by the Senior Advisor. *"Ye Are the Salt of the Earth, but if the salt have lost its savour, wherewith shall it be salted. It in thenceforth good for nothing, but to be cast out and to be trodden underfoot of me. Ye are the light of the world. A city that is set on an hill cannot be hid"* (*Matthew 5:13-14*).

I look back and see that God was making a way for me because of my mother's prayers for us and with us through our formative years. When you take care of God's business, such as having a real relationship with Him, talking to Him daily, fasting, increasing your prayer life, and being faithful to the church as you are to Facebook and other social media apps, God will honor you and your loved ones. Your concerns will become His concerns when the fullness of time shall come. God will give you endurance and patience to wait for the manifestation of the thing or things you desire. Do your part and God will surely do His. He has and owns it all. *"For every beast of the forest is mine, and the cattle upon a thousand hills. I know all the fowls of the mountains and the wild beasts of the field are mine. If I were hungry, I would not tell thee, for the world is mine and the fullness thereof"* (*Psalm 50:10-12*). Who wouldn't serve a God like this?

My church acknowledged my accomplishment in a tangible way and some members of the church as well. I was still looking further to greener pastures in terms of going to college. I knew my parents were not going to let me go off to college. I could only attend the events in the city of Memphis, not Arkansas or Mississippi. It was a closed case before I could even consider it. Finally, I was glad to tell everyone I was enrolled in college. This was another milestone. Lae University, here I come. I had finally made it to a young adult, called womanhood. I could now make my own decisions, just as long as I could live by the decisions I made. I could get my own driver's license, vote, go out of town on my own, and even have a boyfriend. What! "A boyfriend!" Are you serious! I could open my own credit card, get a job, buy a car, dye my hair, hang out a little later, not too late, but within reason. I no longer had a leash tied around my neck. I was free, free, free. No more chains holding me. I guarantee you, if you raise your children up in the fear and admonition of God, it is only so much they are going to do or get into without feeling condemned. I have always been outgoing and happy. I always knew how far to go, in all my different circles. I had always been the leader of the pack. I was bold and never met a stranger. I always lived with a big smile.

My freshman year in college was all about getting to know myself. Man, did I meet a lot of people from various high schools. I had two friends that graduated with me from my old high school. We were like three peas in a pod. We were called the boxy twins even though there were three of us. We were always together, took all our classes together, we even resembled each other in appearance and shared similar opinions, leading some to call us the Bobbsey twins. We would dress alike, hang out in the study hall together, and eat on the same lunch schedule. If you saw one, you saw the others. We basically made the same grades. We were good at sharing notes. *"But when the fullness of time was come" (Galatians 4:4a).* **God had a set time and an appointed time for me.**

Unlike grade school, middle school, and high school, I was very, very popular. My clothes stood out because I worked at the Post Office and made big money like the people who were married with a family. My clothes and shoes came from boutiques and high-end stores. No one had clothes and shoes like mine because money was so, so plentiful for me. I dressed like a CEO of a company with a churchy swag. Therefore, I had a mixture of both styles in one. My clothes were specialty clothes with a flair. **My fullness of time had come.** My shoes had odd heels that no one had ever seen before. I was only 19 years old, but dressed like I had oil wells pumping in my backyard. I never got a big head or became prideful; I always remembered where I came from. I knew the same way the Lord blessed me; He could also take it away. Mind you, my first job was sacking groceries at Kroger. I can hear the manager ringing in my ears, "All sackers on front, All sackers on front." I was so proud to be a sacker at Kroger. I met so many people as I was putting their groceries in bags. God gave me favor with my manager, and he moved me to being a cashier. My line would be so long because the customers loved me. I wore bright colors and always had a smile on my face. It's amazing how the simplest things in life can bring happiness and joy to people. Even now, at age 67, I continue to embrace this approach. It brought joy to people back then, and it continues to do so today. I just added pearls to my attire.

That was my first job during my non-career, humble beginnings. But eventually I had to quit because it took away from my studying time. I will never forget that job. Afterwards, I went on to the Post Office, which is now known as the Bulk Mail Center. I worked from 5 pm to 1 am. I would wear rollers in my hair covered with an oversized scarf, always coordinating with my attire. There was no way I could walk away from money like that. *No way Hosea!* My uncle got my friends and I on out there and we were working as temporary help since it was a new business in Memphis. Those hundreds and thousands of dollars lasted me through college. I was able to pay for everything except my college tuition. Whenever I made the Dean's List, the school would pay my tuition. The Lord opened so many doors for me at that school. *"But when the fullness of time was come" (Galatians 4:4a).* **God had a set time and an appointed time for me to experience, due to my academics."**

My math professor asked if I would be interested in tutoring in Statistics and getting paid through work study, and he would write it up to that effect. I immediately smiled and said, "Yes!" without hesitation. Look at God! I was a mediocre math student in high school now tutoring upper-level Math, Statistics, finding the standard deviation on a college level and getting paid for it. It was God that quicken my understanding and blessed me to catch on quickly. There were many more students in my math class who were smarter than me because they would always turn their tests in so quickly, while I was still working on my test. *The race is not given to the swift, nor the battle to the strong, but the one that endured till the end.* Even if you are not the smartest, strongest, most knowledgeable, or the best looking, God will still give you good success when you depend on His Grace. The acronym for the word Grace is, "God's Riches at Christ's Expense." God's grace is defined as unmerited or underserved favor. I thank God for His favor and mercy. I was also chosen to be "Miss Senior." When you open the yearbook of the class of 1978, I am on the first page standing by a Rolls Royce and a dog. I never asked for that and never would have thought of that. The Senior Advisor gave me that honor. I was shocked to hear it and they never told me I would be on the inside cover of the yearbook. *"God had an auspicious time and momentous time for my life."* I had to go through my childhood experiences and high school, so it would come to pass. When people see you being successful and blessed, they do not know the story behind the glory. It matters not how you start out, but how you end.

While in college, I joined Delta Sigma Theta Sorority. I was able to pay all my fees and purchase all of my uniforms that we stepped in. I bought my own car, a 500 Galaxy, maroon and gray. God gave me so many successes because I kept the faith. I went to church every Sunday and paid my tithes off everything. God would really stretch my money. I loved paying my tithes and offerings, because it was amazing how God would stretch my money and always kept my pocketbook full. Whenever they needed someone to represent the class or department, they would always call on me.

I also joined the Drama Club there and became a Most Noble Thespian. We would take several trips to present our plays. That was such a wonderful experience, even though we never made it to Broadway in New York. In doing all of this, my grades never dropped. I did everything my professors told me to do. I was always a person that stayed focused. I never let the good or unpleasant things alter my steps. I have never wanted my circumstances to determine me. I have always wanted to be in control of my actions, in terms of how I handle unforeseen circumstances. I never took to illegal drugs substances. Although students around me did, that was never my desire or a "let me try it one time" thing. I give God the glory and honor because Paul said, *"But by the grace of God I am what I am"* (1 *Corinthians 15:10).*

God will put people in your life to speak blessings upon you or even prophesize. My best friend once asked me what I wanted to do for a career, I immediately answered and said, "an Executive Secretary traveling with my boss." I did not know what I was saying at 19. I just saw all that on TV. Back then, it looked glamorous to me. I didn't realize the pitfalls that traveling around the country with a man could lead to. Flying together, staying in the same hotel, eating together, and handling business together can open up a whole world of troubles. Both parties can be innocent and content with their personal lives or circumstances. You need to remember, satan is watching and lurking. *"For all that is in the world, the lust of the flesh, and the lust of the eyes, and the pride of life, is not of the Father, but is of the world. And the world passeth away, and the lust thereof, but he that doeth the will of God abideth for ever"* (I John 2:16-17).

I thank God she spoke into my life and said, if you would become a teacher, you will always have a job. When she said that, it was like my head and my heart accepted that immediately. "Yes, Lord." A teacher I will become. My dad would always say, "You would like to have a job you can retire from, not shutting down or leaving the city." He said, "You want to be able to hold the job life-long, career-wise." So many people cannot keep a job or are always job hopping.

I had almost waited too late to get my student-teaching in. I had to take so many hours to have enough credits to graduate, because student teaching gave me twenty-one credit hours and I needed just a few more in math and education. *"But when the fullness of time was come"* (Galatians 4:4a). **God had an auspicious time and momentous time for my life. The**

fullness of time and momentous time underscores God's incursion into time with His answer for people.

I spent seven weeks student teaching at my former high school. I did student teaching under my typing teacher who really liked me and would always give me "E's" in conduct and my friends would always get "S's" in conduct, although they would be talking to each other. Then I took morning classes on campuses that would satisfy my major for graduation. Everything flowed together because God was in it, and I was student teaching under my former high school teacher. It is always good to have a good name and reputation because you never know when you will have to reach back or go back for assistance.

My professor worked everything out for me. He handled all the paperwork and made sure I met the qualifications needed for my BS Degree. God was in it *"My times are in your hand" (Psalm 31:15)*. I received an "A" in student teaching and "A's & B's" in my other educational and math courses. God ordained me to be a teacher before I was born. *"Before I formed thee in the belly, I knew thee, and before thou camest forth out of the womb I sanctified thee, and I ordained thee a prophet unto the nations" (Jeremiah 1:5).*

CHAPTER TWO
Bad Times Are in God's Hands

I did a very, very foolish thing, which could have tarnished my career and could have caused my degree to be delayed. It was coming to the end of my high school year, and they were having Christmas parties all throughout the school. My student teaching mentor put me over the Christmas party for that class. One of the male students in the class worked at Kroger. As we were getting the food together, we were short on a few things. He asked if he could go to Kroger where we worked together to get the items needed. Kroger was not far from the school. I knew he could drive, but I never questioned him about his driver's license. I gave him the keys to my car without permission from the principal, my mentor, or his mom. "I GAVE HIM PERMISSION," end of story, so I thought. I never thought about the what-ifs. I only had my mind on one thing and that was getting the items needed to have a grand Christmas Party. He was gone for more than the time that was expected. We were still organizing and getting things together. The office called me down and said I had an important call. It was the student on the other end telling me that he was in a wreck because after he left Kroger, he headed to his girlfriend's school to pick her up to bring her to the party as a cousin. I told my best friend, who was student teaching with me, what happened. She told me to call my boyfriend, who lived only 3 minutes away, to come and pick me up to carry me to the scene of the accident and to tell the office I had a home emergency. I left school after my boyfriend arrived and hurried to the scene. The student was so hurt and embarrassed. He was speechless because I trusted him. Somehow, I never got upset with him. I was just happy that he was not hurt, and the car was not badly damaged. There was no ticket given and the other person left the scene before we got there. My boyfriend said, "Aretha, it is something that you are doing, and it is not right." I knew that was the Lord speaking to me through him. I took heed later down the road. I broke up with him and started following the Lord wholeheartedly a few months after graduation. *"My times are in God's hand" (Psalm 31:15).*

No one at the school found out, not my principal, the office, my mentor, or the student's parents. It was a hush, hush thing because we were all wrong. He could have gotten suspended, and they could have said that I was not ready to be a teacher and that they wanted me off the campus and to never come back. God! God! God covered me in my immunity and ignorance. I never knew what had become of the Christmas Party and never asked any questions and no one ever asked me any questions. My professor never got wind of it. I thank God for His love and mercy towards me. Even though I was a wretch undone, God knew my future. Who would not serve a God like this? That incident could have haunted me throughout my career and it could have been put into my file at the board. I could have been blackballed.

A few months later, I graduated with not only honors, but my dignity. After graduation, I applied to become a math teacher. Meanwhile, I worked at city hall from the summer after graduation until the fall semester. Still, I never received a call from the Board of Education about the incident.

I enjoyed working at city hall for the Police Department with the white-collar workers. I was 20 years old, and I felt like I had arrived working in the insurance department there. I wore my office wardrobe, hosiery, and heels. I felt very important. I put color in my hair, blondish blonde. I had the eyes of everybody with my God-given smile, fresh out of college. I knew that job was not my career or future. I was just passing through. *Man, did I not enjoy the ride.* Finally, a principal from one of the high schools in Southwest Memphis called me and asked if I could take on the position of a long-term year substitute teacher while the regular teacher was out on maternity leave. He mentioned I would be teaching accounting, spreadsheets, and more. I immediately said yes! He informed me that I would start shortly after Thanksgiving break. I was so excited for my opportunity to teach. *"But when the fullness of time was come" (Galatians 4:4a).* **God had a set time and an appointed time for me to experience and take part in each event He had for me.** I was 21 and my students were 16, 17, and 18. I was only three, four and five years older than my students. It was my one mind teaching thirty other minds. Only God could create such a thing. My classroom was right next to a tenured teacher, who was a member of my brother's church. She really, really helped and nurtured me. Of course, God strategically put me next door. I learned so much from her and stayed connected with her throughout my career. She was a science teacher, and I was a math teacher. She helped me in so many facets. She told me that I was a tremendous help to her because she was so strait laced. She told me how she admired how the students liked me, even the ones I did not teach and how the principals catered to me. She said I knew how to win the principals over because I grew up with a father and she did not. I begged to differ. It was the favor of God upon my life and because my mother took us to prayer meetings, instead of enrolling us into kindergarten and prayed with us in the home. Those prayers over our heads blessed us in so many ways and facets of our lives. She told me not to play with the students so they could always have respect for me and do not smile until after February. I took heed just a little, but as time went on, I saw that what she was telling me was true. Plus, I was told the same things at our departmental meetings and at our district seminars. Those little high school boys had crushes on me. However, I did not pay them any mind. I knew it was just growing pains for them, but they never crossed any boundaries with me. There was one young lady who challenged me. But God took part in the end. She ran for Miss Monticello High and won the majority of the votes from the entire school. But the senior advisor and Principal would not give her the title. When she performed her talent, she got down on the floor with a young man as if she were making out with him. They said that kind of behavior was not appropriate, and she was not fitting to carry the title or the name of the school. The only thing we have to do is hold our peace and God will fight for you. After losing the title, she was quiet and humble for the rest of the year. God has the final say. She was jealous because the male students gave me a lot of attention.

She was a pretty young lady but was missing something. Eventually, she really clung to me and wanted to go home with me.

I made it through that school year, and I would give myself a B- because I thought it was ok for students to "check" each other. But I learned that some students would go too far with it. My mentor next door told me this, but I had to learn the hard way. It is good to have an ear to hear, especially when you are a novice. One thing about being a teacher, you always have another chance to start over the next school year and learn from your past mistakes. Every school year, you will have a new set of students to experiment with as you teach and also learn along the way. I made it through my first school year of teaching math. The principal who hired me got promoted to assistant principal at my former school. He admired how I had good control of my students and did not have to write up students every day. God gave me the solution for discipline. He told me to pray and fast, and I would see the results. I did that and saw results instantaneously as a very young teacher. He told me to stay in my classroom or cafeteria. Do not hang in the teacher's lounge during my planning period or lunchtime. I obeyed. The teacher's lounge was a gripe room where teachers discussed and complained about their students, administration, other colleagues and sometimes politics. God knows. I did not need to be in that kind of setting day after day. He had already given me the keys and tools to keep my sanity and peace. *"Depart from evil, and do good. Seek peace and pursue it. The eyes of the Lord are upon the righteous and his ears are open until they unto their cry" (Psalm 34:14-15).* I would go into the lounge five minutes earlier before the bell would ring so no one would stop and try to detain me. As you know, misery loves company. Every now and then I would get stopped. That is when my "acting" would kick in. They would say, "Terry, what do you think?" or "How would you feel about such and such?" I would respond with things like, "Which girl?" or "Really?" This kept them at a distance because I didn't engage or address the issue as they expected me to. They would reply, "Terry, you are so naïve." I would walk away and say to myself, "Thank you, Jesus, it worked." I wanted to avoid being involved in any he said, she said, they said, or Terry said situations. I had peace and favor on my job. I was not going to let satan snatch it from me. *"Surely He shall deliver you from the snare of the fowler and from the noisome pestilence" (Psalm 91:3).* These are used metaphorically to remind us that God is able to protect and care for His people in any situation. It also represents both hidden and visible dangers that Christians or the Body of Christ encounters throughout their daily activities. God delivers His people from the snare (a trap set by Satan). He does not let you get in it. Like when God told me not to hang out in the teacher's lounge which was directly across from my classroom. That is why you might not know the reasons or the ins and outs. Just obey and you will understand it better by and by.

When one is disobedient with His mercy, He will still deliver you, but you will have to go through some things that you normally would not have to. I had a friend who was a follower of Christ, deeply. I shared with her what the Lord had told me, but she did not take heed. I told her that too much goes on in the teacher's lounge, which can turn out to be very messy. I told her that they do a lot of carnal talk about everything from A to Z. She said, "I just like to be in there to know what is going on around the school. I barely give any input, I just listen." "*Blessed is the man that walketh not in the counsel of the ungodly, nor standeth in the way of sinners, nor sitteth in the seat of the scornful*" (Psalm 1:1). "*But his delight is in the Law of the Lord, and in His law doth he meditate day and night*" (Psalm 1:2). Well, her colleagues knew she was different and that her personality as well as her character did not fit in with them. She kept going anyway until she was run out. They played a big, embarrassing trick on her. One of the coaches gave her a Christmas gift from the other colleagues in there and himself. She thought it was so nice of them to get together and give her a gift. She accepted the gift and told them she would open it on Christmas day. They insisted that she open it then, so they could see her reaction. As she opened the gift, the room was extremely quiet and the coach who presented it to her told her, "We know you are going to be very busy for the holiday and we just wanted to give you this to relax you." She opened it in front of everyone. It was a "dildo" an artificial erect penis! She was so embarrassed that she cried and ran out of the lounge. She never went back there again to congregate. Sometimes, God must step in and help us. She was a super sensitive person. She told me her whole Christmas Break was just terrible, to be reminded how they all got together to do her like that. It is always good in life to take heed; a hint to the wise is always sufficient. I also learned from her mistake. I taught school for 35 years and I never had an interest in being a lounge hound.

Life is easy when you learn from other people's mistakes. I know we have always heard, "Experience is the best teacher," but they never added the other part to that adage, "Experience is the best teacher, but only fools go to that school." What the adage is simply saying is, in life you can learn from other's mistakes, not only from your own experience, but theirs.

CHAPTER THREE
My Times Are in God's Hands

T he principal who was promoted from assistant to principal took me to his new school, which was on the Northwest side of town. It was the biggest junior high school in the state of Tennessee. Ninety percent of the students at the school were from the projects. I would say that ten percent were being raised by their grandmothers. Those students were so worldly, unchurched, street smart, in gangs, or sold drugs. What was a blessing was that only two percent of them had babies. Well, God sent me there for a two-fold purpose; to understand and learn life from the students and they would learn math and God from me. We both had a lot to bring to the table to feed each other. It was not planned by either side. Now that I have retired and looking back in retrospect, God had me on a mission, unbeknownst to me. I could freely talk about God because the principal was a devout Christian. The students would always bring up religion because they would ask questions or ask my opinion; it was legal. I would not bring it up or start a conversation about it. These students were very open-minded to the unknown. I also had the opportunity to instill values, morals, and teach etiquette along the way. The students loved math. They said I

34

knew how to break it down and make it extremely easy to learn. Some would say that they never understood or liked math until the year I taught them. I would drill and reinforce, until they got it, and they would have the opportunity to go to the board and explain their problem step by step. This would build their self-esteem and give them the opportunity to be seen for something positive, rather than checking each other and putting each other down. For every positive thing they would say, not being planned, they would get a point. I thank God for always giving me how to work and teach adolescent children.

Whatever went on in the neighborhood, it was always brought to school. God had to really give me the wisdom on how to administer to an unknown culture. I was only 22 and sheltered. God always create an opportunity for us to get closer to Him. *"Draw nigh to God and he will draw nigh to you" (James 4:8).* When we get closer to God, you will build a day-to-day relationship. The same way you want to hear from your best friend or significant other. God wants to hear from us through prayer, which is when we are talking to Him; through reading His Word, which is when He is talking to us. Sometimes you need answers, directions, and have decisions to make. He will give it to you right in His Word. God will respond by moving closer to us. That is a merciful God. We know the God of the universe owes us nothing, not even His closeness to us. Here are some other things I learned throughout my career: to foster a greater relationship with God, give thanks in all things, practice humility, memorize scriptures in the Bible and quote them throughout the day, know that your body is not your own, your body is the temple of the Holy Ghost, and do not forget to start and end your day with God in case you do not wake up. Always quote the Lord's prayer, that way you have asked the Lord for forgiveness, for commission and omission. That is the repentance prayer, and we can still make it in if we do not wake up.

I remember animosity had begun to rise among the different projects and I could feel the tension. I said I needed to pray in this room, during my planning period, which lasted an hour, and I did. I cut the lights off and moved over to a corner with my door locked and began to pray. In just that little scant time, I saw a difference in their behavior and attitudes toward each other. God made a believer out of me about the power of prayer. I opened the Bible and God let my eyes fall on this scripture, *"And the Lord said unto him, I have heard the prayer and thy supplication, that thou hast made before me. I have hallowed this house, which thy has built, to put my name there forever, and mine eyes and mine heart shall be there perpetually." (1 Kings 9:3).* When I read that, it was like the Lord was speaking to me audibly. My heart was so encouraged just when He said in that scripture, *"I have thy prayer and supplication."* To me, God was saying, He had accepted my prayers. God was letting me know He was granting His presence. God let me know that He was watching over me and protecting me if I continued to worship Him. I was 23 years old and that was some kind of manifestation.

My students were so nice to each other, they were not hostile, they were glad to meet up in my room. They told me the other classes and teachers were different from me. They knew there was a difference but did not know what it was. I felt good just for them to fathom the difference. They began to ask more questions about Math, without feeling dumb or that someone was going to check them. It was a joyous day with all my classes. I could see the manifestation when God said, *"mine eyes and mine heart shall be thee perpetually,"* which meant continuously. My faith began to increase more. I saw the true meaning of reading God's Word. Your answer to everything is in the Bible. We must dust it off and read it daily. Yes, it is a humbling thing, ask God to give you the mind to read His Word and run references on it. It teaches, reproves, corrects, and trains us in righteousness. We will be able to look at life through the lens of the Word of God. My times are in God's hand.

I noticed my students started to care more about their appearance and put on cologne. They made sure their hair was fixed and the young men would have their hair lined. When God blesses you, he blesses everything that pertains to you. *"And the ark of the LORD continued in the house of Obededom the Gittite three months: and the LORD blessed Obededom, and all his household. And it was told king David, saying, The LORD hath blessed the house of Obededom, and all that pertaineth unto him, because of the ark of God. So, David went and brought up the ark of God from the house of Obededom into the city of David with gladness"* (2 Samuel 6:11-12).

That is why it is so important to read the Word and know the Word therefore you can declare and decree it in your life.

CHAPTER FOUR
God is No Respecter of Persons

Whatever God did for Peter, James, John, or anyone in the Bible, He will do the same for us. God said try me and see, that I will pour you out a blessing that you will not have room to receive. The students felt really good about going to the chalkboard and explaining their problems. The other students would praise them, and I would give out candy. A good time was had by all. Satan would try to rise up every now and then, but he did not get the victory. No weapon formed against us shall prosper. God said He had hallowed this house. Which means He had honored my classroom. The devil in hell cannot win against God. He is going to try, because he has power, and he is mighty. God is Almighty, Case Closed! Nothing else to be said. I love one of the names of God, El Roi, Thy God seest me. Not only that, but He also knows me, He hears me, He cares for me, above all, He loves me, so dearly. I appreciate God for allowing us to have a personal relationship with Him. We have access to Him 24 hours a day. He never sleeps nor slumbers. *"Behold, he that keepeth Israel shall neither slumber nor sleep" (Psalm 121:4).* We cannot find a friend or relative that we can depend on nor lean on 24/7. Everything we have, we can put it all in God's hand. In Him we live, we move and have our being.

The principal of the school was a God-fearing, unrelenting man who served as a father figure in every aspect. For many students, he filled the role of father, especially since they came from single-parent households—often with only a mother or grandmother present.

The students looked up to him and respected him. He was the positive male role model that was missing out of their homes. They would spend more time at school than they would awake at home. He knew he was making a difference in their lives. He treated them with love and respect. God knew that these students needed a firm principal, who showed love, care, and respect for them daily. I thank God, He chose me to be in their lives as well, as a positive role model. Even though I was sheltered growing up, God gave me how to mix and mingle so that the students knew that I cared. My caring came from deeds not just talk. They had heard talk all their childhood, but when would be the time when the talk and action would intertwine? The students participated in field trips, clubs, the student government association, special luncheons for students that excelled in their grades, and received free passes to the dances. The students made a 180° degree turnaround. Everything was smelling like roses. Parents became more involved and visible. Every now and then we would have fathers that would come out of the woodwork, sort of speak. The principal had a good name in the community with how he changed the atmosphere of the school and how he cleaned up Northside Memphis. That was the second school I had taught in at the age of 23 years old. I had really gotten a lot of experience from these two schools, but little did I know, I had so much more to learn and grasp. Those two years at that particular school went by so fast. Time actually flies when you are having a good time.

My principal called me over the summer and told me they were promoting him to high school, to another North Memphis school and asked me if I was available and wanted to go. With no hesitation I remarked a big, "Yes!" I knew where he would be the principal, the school would definitely be under control. I could feel free expressing my walk with God to the children and elaborate whenever they would ask questions.

I was back with the high school during my fourth year of teaching. These students were basically from the projects as well, but overall, they had a brighter outlook, and their self-esteem was good for the most part. Although these students were from across the track, they were different in a positive way. Their manners were good and easy to get along with. I started a club from young ladies of all grades and named it, "Ladies Unlimited." I wrote an Easter play and the students performed it at a church in South Memphis. The title was *"I'm not waiting on the Easter bunny; I'm waiting on God."* It was a big hit, and we had several sponsors. I was a most noble thespian in college, so it was easy for me to write and carry out. I have always enjoyed speaking and acting. My best friend tells me even as of now, "You are still acting, and it comes so easily for you." And it does. I taught those girls etiquette, morals, how to meet and greet people, how to respect their elders, when to hold and when to fold, how to attack personal hygiene, how to take care of their skin, and much more. I was their mom away from home. I was implementing reiteration. None of my students had babies unlike other high schools I taught in. That was just a phenomenal school year and class. Especially coming from that area. *"And Nathanael said unto him, can there be any good thing come out of Nazareth? Phillip saith unto him, come and see. And he saith unto him, Verily, Verily, I say unto you thereafter ye shall see heaven open, and the angels of the God ascending and descending upon the son of man" (John 1:46,51).* I really, really enjoyed working under that principal. During the Black History Program I was over, we honored him and invited a special speaker and had several big wigs from the district and the Board of Education. When school ended that day, all the teachers and other colleagues gave him a private party at his favorite restaurant. I did not know that would be the last year I would be teaching under his auspices. *"But when the fullness of time was come" (Galatians 4:4a).* **God had a set time and an appointed time for me to experience and take part in each event.**

CHAPTER FIVE
I Didn't Understand God's Timing

I did not know that the celebration I had for the principal during Black History month would be my departure appreciation celebration for him. Well, my time was up for following him to his new schools. I learned so much as a young new teacher. He exposed me to so much in my early twenties. I taught Jr. High and High School students, mathematics. That is when I realized my passion was for high school students and upper-level math courses. I left school that day knowing I would not work under him anymore. I realized I wouldn't have that secure crutch or someone to look after me, at least that's what I thought and harbored in my mind. That was an incredibly sad, emotional day for me, as I drove off the lot. That day seemed so dark to me. I felt like I was leaving the security package of my career behind. I knew I was a long-term substitute teacher, but I had and did more than the teachers that were certified. The teacher I was substituting for was returning. I knew it was all in God's hands, but I did not want to accept it. I took my teacher certification test and passed on my first attempt. I was content going from school to school, getting great experiences and meeting new teachers. I am a people's person. We will never understand God's timing, but it is always for our good. *"And we know that all things work together for good to those who love God to those who are the called according to his purpose" (Romans 8:28).* The Board of Education sent me to Riley High. This was something new for me. The principal was my high school teacher and was a Caucasian gentleman, unlike what I had in previous years. The population of the students were multicultural, unlike all Black students from my previous schools. The students spoke several languages and English was their second language. The school was shaped like a dome and all classes were on one floor. Every day we were going in circles. A play on words, but literally, I had a lot to learn, visualize, and see where I would fit in. All my crutches were gone. I was on my own. But I can honestly say, where God guides, He will provide. They saw me as something different too. I dressed up every day; no jeans or slacks on me. I wore heels and makeup every day. Occasionally, I wore my wigs. My students would always ask, "Why do you put on a wig with all that hair you have?" I replied, "Sometimes, I don't feel like rolling my hair at night, sometimes I have bad hair days, and sometimes my outfits would call for short hair." I was definitely a fashionista and have been since my college days. Appearance means everything. People often treat you the way you present yourself. When you fix yourself up daily, it makes you look like you have money. Look at what the Bible says, *"For wisdom is a defence and money is a defence, but the excellence of knowledge is that wisdom gives life to those who have it" (Ecclesiastes 7:12).*

Many days I would be sharp as a tack and wouldn't have a dime in my pocketbook, but who knew. My appearance said otherwise. I was told never to expose a person, cover them. Same thing with me because I did not have any money. I did not want to dress or look like I didn't. I did not expose myself, I covered myself through fixing myself up from head to toe. God gives you wisdom how to go in and out before people, like Solomon asked for. *"Give me now wisdom and knowledge, that I may go out and come in before this people" (II Chronicles 2:10a).* I was still a young girl in my eyes, 25 years old. One mind teaching 150 minds a day, only God can produce a phenomenal gift like that.

I met all my students for the first time, this was a big task for me, unlike what I was used to. My classroom consisted of many nationalities along with their interpreters. I had to learn their traditions, religions, and customs. Discipline was not an issue there. They were very humble students and were glad to be in America, Home of the Free and Brave. They understood very little English, but they were willing to catch on fast and they did before the school year ended. Their interpreters could speak both languages and could really translate it. The only thing I had to do was to pronounce their names and I have always been good with spelling and phonetics. Once they would tell me their name, I would write it in my roll book the way it sounded in English phonetically. My math advisor would visit me every six weeks. She was ecstatic that I could pronounce their names so plainly in their language. God game me how to write it phonetically. I had a lot of students that had the name, "Nguyen." It was pronounced nothing like it was spelled. It was pronounced as "Win." God gave me to write it exactly the way it was pronounced, and my advisor did not know I had translated it in my roll book as the way it sounded rather than spelled. God gave that real quick. That is why we need to talk to God every day like a natural man or as your father. *"For in him we live and move, and have our being, as certain also of your own parts have said. For we are his offspring" (Acts 17:28).* It is a wonderful thing to be led by God. He will give you ideas and knowledge that you know wholeheartedly that God gave it to you. It pays to have day-to-day contact with Him. We sure are going to need Him.

My advisor was very, very old school. Many math teachers did not care for her, but she loved me. She would remark on how I dressed so professionally and was good for today's students and their parents. She would always put me on program at the beginning of the school year after summer break. They would get me to welcome all the math teachers in the city or do the occasion. This was a very high honor for me, being extremely young, a novice, and not having made tenure yet. This would be in front of six hundred math teachers across Memphis City Schools. I was definitely in my element when it came to speaking and acting. I knew how to project my voice, use present cliches, stand with great posture, and scan the crowd with my eyes. The bigger the crowd, the better I could speak. Was I nervous, YES, but all of that helped me to really pronounce and articulate because all eyes were on me. I am not trying to pin roses on my shoulder, but many times the keynote speaker was boring and spoke in a monotone voice. My speech and drama teacher spoke against this daily. You never want to bore your audience or put them to sleep or get them to get lost in their cell phones because of boredom.

Things were really working out for me. I received great evaluations from my principal and my math advisor. My students enjoyed the way I taught math with simplicity and the interpreters did also. It was a good time, a new learning experience mixed with diversity. Things were working out so smoothly and fast. I had forgotten all about my past three schools and the principal. Paul said, *"Brethren, I do not count myself to have apprehended, but one thing I do, forgetting those things which are behind and reaching forward to those things which are ahead" (Phillipians 3:13).* I was growing up and had become a big girl now. I was on my own in the natural, but spiritually so, I was wrapped up in the palm of the Lord's hand, from the time I left home and upon returning.

One day, my principal called me into his office and asked if I had received my call from the board. I replied and said, "No, I have not." He said, "Wait a minute." He then proceeded to call the Board of Education in front of me and blasted the person in HR. It was the end of the year going into the second semester. They sent me to Harvey High. I had the opportunity to meet the teacher I was succeeding. She told me I would be the fifth teacher for that same class in one semester. I could look at her and knew the students had carried her through the hackles. She was dressed like she was going to hang clothes on the line and her face was saying, "Please get me out, Jesus." When I saw her, it felt like fear was ready to take over me. The main thing, I was a certified math teacher for k-12, had administration certification, business certification, and education. I had various avenues with privileges. God instilled in me high school math, which is where I started and ended after 35 years. Did I try to venture out? Yes, I did, and was successful. God was not in the plan, so it did not prosper or last. The safest place is in the will of God. Doing things on your own or because you can, will not prosper if God is not in it. He might let you go and test the water, but you will not be able to stay.

I had another principal who really wanted me badly to teach his second graders. I had my doubts, but I said, "Why not?" I can go back to math any time of the year, at the beginning of the year, the middle of the year, even the end of the year. There is always a great demand for math teachers. I told the principal of Bedrock Elementary School that I would love to come. I had about twenty little second graders. They always wanted to be on the floor, wanted to tell me something, wanted to tell me what they had for dinner, what their parents were going to buy them, what was going on in their homes, show me their news shoes, new outfits; just any and everything to get my attention. I felt like getting my purse and running to my car and not looking back. A good name means more than anything. *"A good name is to be chosen rather than great riches, loving favor rather than silver and gold" (Proverbs 22:1).* The students wanted to pat on you all day, asking can they lead the lunch line, could they pass out the lunch tickets, could they lead the line going to the restroom, could they lead the line coming back from lunch, or could they lead the line to the playground? I was not used to this kind of culture. I would just yes, to get them out of my face and to stop patting on me. Then another group would ask the same questions the next day. Again, I would say, yes, to get them out of my face. They would go back to wherever they were, with a big smile on their face and tell the other students I said they could do thus and so. When the time came for me to call on someone, I would pick the one who did not ask, who was not in my face or patting on me all the time. I knew eventually I would get around to everybody. I would look at the students' faces who ask me for the little task, their eyes would be welled up with tears. That did not mean anything to me, because I have never been a lover of little spoiled brats. That was the end of that, or so I thought.

The next morning, two or three parents would send me notes reprimanding me, telling me not to promise or tell the students something and then change. I was not bothered one bit. Students would all ask the same questions, at the same time, and I would answer them the same way because again, I would give all of them an opportunity before the year end. I felt like it was the parents' responsibility to tell his or her child, "Let the teacher call on you, you do not have to ask every day." I kept running my class the way I wanted. Finally, the principal who wanted me to come there, called me into the office and reprimanded me and told me I had to conform to second graders and get more involved with them and to not have a "standoff" attitude. I told him I was a high school teacher, and my personality was not for little children. Thanks, but no thanks. I finished that first semester and "got out of dodge!" I was just trying something new. I was not in the will of God. My personality and message were for adolescence. God just had mercy on me. It seemed like a good idea at the time, but it was not a God-inspired idea. It did not work, neither did it last. God let me see that for myself. He helped usher me out and I never looked back. When I passed by there, every blue moon, it was like I never worked on the campus or ever driven my car there. I always let it be known, I want all my students to be 16-19 years old. By then, they know the meaning of an education and graduation. Every now and then you still will have some on "fool's hill."

High school, here I come! I wholeheartedly knew my calling and my niche. Life is not about what we want for our lives but is about what God wants for our lives. We were all made for a purpose. *"Even Jesus had to be in the will of God, saying, 'Father, if thou be willing, remove this cup from me:*

nevertheless not my will, but thine, be done'" (Luke 22:42). I found out in life we should prioritize what God wants for our lives and be willingly open as He guides us on paths we may not have pictured ourselves on. God has a purpose for each of us, even when we do not understand, and it is much better than the plans that we could form in our hearts. The same way the holy spirit does not resist God, let the body not resist the holy spirit. Sometimes, God will let us choose our own path in certain situations like Jonah did. God allowed Jonah to be in the belly of a big fish for three days. Once the fish vomited him out, Jonah obeyed God and left for Nineveh right away. It was a three-day journey, but Jonah did it all in one day. God made things very uncomfortable for Jonah, until he was in the will of God! *"Then Jonah prayed unto the Lord his God out of the fish's belly, and said, I cried by reason of mine affliction unto the Lord, and he heard me; out of the belly of hell cried I, and thou headrest my voice. But I will sacrifice unto thee with the voice of thanksgiving; I will pay that that I have vowed. Salvation is of the Lord. And the Lord spake unto the fish, and it vomited out Jonah upon the dry land" (Jonah 2:1,2, 9-10).* *"But when the fullness of time was come" (Galatians 4:4a).* Jonah and I both knew to say, "Yes, Lord, not my will but thine will be done."

CHAPTER SIX
The Omnipotent

God is all powerful and almighty. Anytime I would move and go to another school, they would give me three schools to choose from, because math teachers are hard to find. Those that have math degrees usually venture out in corporate America, where they can make more money rather than chase behind a bunch of students. They would rather become engineers, statisticians, research analyst, accountants, actuary, economist, aeronautical engineer, and so forth. Those professionals' work essentially involves using math skills, and they made six figures. When you are in the will of God, making just five figures or nearly six figures is based on how many degrees you have. God is all powerful and almighty. When you are a strict tithe payer and offering prayer according to Malachi 3: 10-12, *"Bring ye all the tithes into the storehouse, that there may be meat in mine house, and prove me now herewith, saith the Lord of hosts, if I will not open you the windows of heaven..."* not doors, a house has more windows than doors, *"...and pour you out a blessing that there shall not be room enough to receive it."* During and after the pandemic, I received so much food. I fed twelve families on my street and I'm still distributing food to six families as I am writing my second book. I have three freezers and still don't have room enough to store my food. During Christmas, I contributed to 20 Christmas baskets. *"And I will rebuke the devourer for your sakes, and he shall not destroy the fruits of your ground, neither shall your vine cast her fruit before the time in the field said the Lord of hosts" (Malachi 3:11)*. It can be anything that is destroying you physically, naturally, emotionally, spiritually, or financially, that can harm you. *"And all nations shall call you blessed, for ye shall be a delightsome land, saith the Lord of hosts" (Malachi 3:12)*. Symbolically, it represents fullness and completeness.

God is all powerful and all knowing. You will never miss out following God. I have tried Him in so many areas, by obeying Him and following Him. The path He chose for me was not my choice at all, but my biggest and phenomenal blessings were predicated on His path for my life. It is really true, "Father knows best." It will bring you pleasure and joy. *"Thou wilt show me the path of life: in thy presence is fullness of joy; at thy right hand there are pleasures for evermore" (Psalm 16:11)*. Walking with God is a major task. We must accept Him as our personal Savior, not our spouse, job, or children. We must listen to God, not our best friends or things we hear on social media. We must trust God not just when everything else fails, but from the very beginning. We should agree with God, not with the status quo or my rights. We must obey God, not every wind and doctrine. Remember, *"In the beginning was the Word and the Word was with God and the Word was God. The same was in the beginning with God" (John 1: 1-2)*. We must walk in the same direction God walks. Sometimes you will get tired and desire to take a big break. Sometimes you would like to pause and go in another direction. We know His direction is the best and it will increase our intimacy with God. We must remember the Omnipotent is in charge and we must praise Him for it.

I had to work at Harvey High, which turned out to be the high school that would mold me and make me, without any crutches from the principals I had at the other schools. I taught upper-level math there, so I knew that the students who chose to take these courses did so by choice and found math relatively unchallenging. However, God allowed a few students to keep me fasting and praying. Man, I am telling you, if you are going through something that is desirable, praying and fasting will bring about peace. God will give you the victory over that giant's head. One of my students had stolen my bookends off my desk. All I said was, "When I find out who you are, you will leave here with the police." He immediately ran to his locker and brought them back wrapped in newspaper. From that point on, I did not have any problems with him or anyone else in the classroom. Oftentimes, the things we go through, our spouse, children, uncertainties on the job, finances, or even our health, sometimes God lets those things appear, because He knows those will be the things that will get our attention. God can fix or correct those things in the blink of an eye. He wants us to reach a place where we are closer to Him. He wants us to grow more spiritually. This includes removing certain habits from our lives, such as lying to impress people or making others think we have it all together when, in reality, we have a broken heart due to a wayward daughter or a disrespectful son whom we did not raise properly. You may not have been wise in your finances and wasted a lot of money on foolish things. Build that strong one on one relationship with God. You will see life differently; you will be able to endure hardness as a good soldier. *The footprints you see in the sand, are not yours, but God's.* He is the one that is carrying you. You do not have the strength or stamina to endure. Paul said, *"Thou therefore endure hardness, as a good soldier of Jesus Christ. No man that warreth entangleth himself with the affairs of this life; that he may please him who hath chosen him to be a soldier. And if a man also strive for masteries, yet is he not crowned, except he strive lawfully"* *(2 Timothy 2:3-5).* We must accept the gracious offer of God to be a part of our lives. By doing so, we will not become discouraged easily. Letting God be the first place in your life will help you get through your tests and trials without compromising or wavering. We must rely on God for everything.

CHAPTER SEVEN
Omniscient

There are a lot of people out there who will proclaim emphatically that they have a relationship with God. "NEWS ALERT!" First of all, a relationship means connection, association, correspondence, or a bond. Let us talk in the natural. For instance, if you have a relationship with a man or woman, you would like to hear from him or her daily. Frequent times, throughout the day and at bedtime really makes it dandy. Your relationship is so strong you think about them throughout the day. You send little emojis on your break and you straight out call or text on your lunch time. On your way home, you would like to hear from them as well, because you want to have a strong relationship. If you do not hear from them all day, you go bananas, because you miss that relationship and feel emptiness or loneliness. You might think, "How could they not text or call me back? Do they have another interest besides me?" Then you panic and your nerves are on edge because you miss that relationship.

Check to see if you have a relationship with God like that. Ask yourself these questions. Do I talk to God every day or just when I am in trouble? Do I cut my radio off in the car and talk to God? Do I talk to Him throughout the day or maybe my day is really busy, and I talk to Him at bedtime when I have a little more time to pour out to Him? Do I think about God throughout the day until it makes me want to open my Bible, so He can speak to me? Do I memorize little scriptures because He is on my mind? Does a day go by, and I realize I feel empty or lonely because I have not spoken to Him all day? If this is not happening, then you know, you do not have a relationship with Him because you are not on speaking terms with Him. Everybody will exclaim, *"I know God or I know the Man."* But He does not know YOU. *"Not every one that saith unto me, Lord, Lord, shall enter into the kingdom of heaven; but he that doeth the will of my Father which is in heaven. Many will say to me in that day, Lord, Lord, have we not prophesied in thy name? and in thy name have cast out devils? and in thy name done many wonderful works? And then will I profess unto them, I never knew you: depart from me, ye that work iniquity"* (Matthew 7:21-23). Many people will say, "I serve the Lord, I believe in the Lord," yet they DO NOT OBEY ANY OF HIS COMMANDMENTS!

"So when they had dined, Jesus saith to Simon Peter, Simon, son of Jonas, lovest thou me more than these? He saith unto him, Yea, Lord; thou knowest that I love thee. He saith unto him, Feed my lambs. He saith to him again the second time, Simon, son of Jonas, lovest thou me? He saith unto him, Yea, Lord; thou knowest that I love thee. He saith unto him, Feed my sheep. He saith unto him the third time, Simon, son of Jonas, lovest thou me? Peter was grieved because he said unto him the third time, Lovest thou me? And he said unto him, Lord, thou knowest all things; thou knowest that I love thee. Jesus saith unto him, Feed my sheep" (John 21:15-17).

God is Omniscient, all knowing and all seeing. Omniscience means God knows everything about all of us in this universe. God knows everything including the past and future. There is nothing God is unaware of. He is everywhere at the same time. God can declare from the beginning how it will end and foretell from the start what has not yet happened. Since God knows all and sees all, He is the only Judge. *"Who art thou that judgest another man's servant? to his own master he standeth or falleth. Yea, he shall be holden up: for God is able to make him stand" (Romans 14:4). "But why dost thou judge thy brother? or why dost thou set at nought thy brother? for we shall all stand before the judgment seat of Christ" (Romans 14:10). "Let us not therefore judge one another any more: but judge this rather, that no man put a stumblingblock or an occasion to fall in his brother's way" (Romans 14:13).*

God should always be first, then family second, your ministry or your passion should be third. Many people have it the other way around. I found out that by putting God first in everything, you will have *"...the peace of God, which surpasses all understanding" (Philippians 4:7)*. This peace that God supplies goes beyond and over the top of any kind of peace. Sometimes, we have the proclivity to find peace in other things, like our career, spouse, money, physical appearance, neighborhood, even wearing or carrying designer things. There is no peace like the peace of God. God's peace is permanent and secure. God's peace doesn't change with the circumstances, it is secure in spite of the circumstances. God's peace is built on the sure foundation of His Word. The world's peace is fleeting and changes with circumstances and is built on the weak foundation of compromise.

During my career, I knew daily that God had to be the head of my life and career. He also had to be the center of my joy. *"These things have I spoken unto you, that my joy might remain in you, and that your joy might be full" (John 15:11).* I found out and learned a lot about God during my career, chasing behind adolescents. The more time I spent with the Lord on a consistent basis, the more I would be in His presence, the more joy I experienced. I remember when my husband walked away from our marriage, I was walking the opposite way of one of my colleagues when she looked at me and said, "Ms. Terry, it doesn't seem like you go through anything." I just smiled, because that was a very, very dark day for me. My husband had just left and I did not share it with anyone on the job because my colleagues thought I had a model marriage by looking at the way I dressed, the vehicle I drove, the big diamond ring, and the mink coats I aways wore. That is what they were made for, to wear and give you warmth, right? However, they were on the outside looking in and were truly judging the book by its cover. Nevertheless, the Lord let that teacher say to me, "it seems like you don't ever go through anything" to let me know He was covering me. The covering that God gave me, the mink coat could not do it. Even though I was hurting and disappointed on the inside, God's covering covered me as if I had it all together. That is why it is important to spend time with the Lord on a consistent basis. Thank God daily for all the wonderful blessings and favor He has bestowed on you. Your peace will overrule any circumstance you are going through. Paul says for us to "Rejoice in hope," because we know deliverance is coming. "Be patient in tribulation," because we all have our own cross to bear. My sister always says, "Everybody has their own row to hoe." Paul says finally, "be constant in prayer, pray without ceasing."

The answer in having joy is giving God the first part of your day, the first priority to every decision and the first place in your heart. *"But seek ye first the kingdom of God, and his righteousness, and all these things shall be added unto you"* *(Matthew 6:33)*. If you do not chase the kingdom of God first, in the end it will make no difference what you have chosen instead. If God is in the right place, a thousand problems can be solved all at once. God is omnipotent—all-powerful and almighty. He is omniscient—all-knowing and all-seeing. He is also omnipresent—always present everywhere.

God has brought joy to my life ever since I have been walking with Him. Natural joy comes from a happening in our lives. Biblical joy is a lasting motion, all the way to eternity that comes from the choice to trust that God will fulfill His promises. We know that God is a promise keeper, so we know our continual walk with Him will keep us with joy and peace no matter what we have experienced in life. I am not talking from what others have said. I lost my sister, my husband, and my mom all within eight days. My mom and my sister were funeralized and buried three days before my husband's funeral. I had joy, peace, contentment, but most of all, I had His Word. I stood on His Word. He will not put any more on you than you can bear. He never makes a mistake. **My times are in God's hand**. When my husband gave up on our marriage, I had peace and contentment, but as the Bible says, "joy cometh in the morning." My joy came every second. That Wednesday, when I drew his social security, it paid my thirteen-room mortgage and one of my luxury vehicles. If you haven't started, get a real relationship with God and pray daily before you leave home and watch God work for you in every facet of your life. God said in His Word, *"For thy Maker is thine husband; the Lord of hosts is his name; and thy Redeemer the Holy One of Israel; The God of the whole earth shall he be called"* (Isaiah 54:5). *"For I am jealous over you with godly jealousy: for I have espoused you to one husband, that I may present you as a chaste virgin to Christ"* (2 Corinthians 11:2).

God is Omniscient, He sees and knows all. *"The eyes of the Lord are in every place, beholding the evil and the good"* *(Proverbs 15:3).* He sees the bad first. Nothing in the world is hidden from God. Everything is uncovered and naked before Him. We must give an account of everything we do. God sees the ends of the earth and sees everything under the heavens. God is aware if every tear you cry. El Roi means thy God seeth me. God is aware of the past, present, and future. Nothing has or ever will surprise God. Many people asked where was God during the pandemic. I am glad you asked. He was sitting on the throne. He could have set up judgement day and ended the whole universe. He loves us so much, until He is waiting for man to connect with him, before He calls them home. God is so merciful; He gives us new mercies every morning. Anything there is to know and all that can be known, God knows it.

CHAPTER EIGHT
Omnipresent

G od is everywhere at the same time. He is all present. There is nothing God cannot do. There is no location where He does not inhabit. God inhabits the entirety of this whole universe. God has unlimited power. My favorite scripture is, *"For the eyes of the Lord run to and fro throughout the whole earth, to shew himself strong in the behalf of them whose heart is perfect toward him"* (2 Chronicles 16:9). *"For the eyes of the Lord are over the righteous, and his ears are open unto their prayers: but the face of the Lord is against them that do evil"* (1 Peter 3:12). God seeth all our goings and pondereth all our goings. I feel very confident to know that God sees, hears, and knows everything about me. People have the tendency to misjudge me because of my story and personality, traits that were inherited from my grandmother and father. My outspokenness was embedded in me by God after being raised in a sheltered environment. I needed that running and chasing adolescents for approximately thirty-five years. God equips us for our task. Where God guides, He will provide.

We cannot fool God or manipulate Him. Once we fully grasp that and understand these truths, we will be able to rest in peace, stand still, and allow God to order our steps with ease and contentment. God allows things in our lives to teach us lessons. He wants us to know who He is and to show us who people really are. Most of the time for us to learn, we have to feel and believe. We have to see for ourselves, like doubting Thomas, one of the apostles. God searches our hearts. He looks deeply inside of us instead of evaluating us by the way we look on the surface. God knows us the way we truly are, not just the way we seem to be. God has access to every thought, every action, and every mistake in our lives. He even knows our motives. Just think, God knows all our business, the good and the bad. God knows the very hairs of our head, because he numbered them.

God knows the inside of us and the outside. He is everywhere at the same time; this can be frightening sometimes as well as comforting. God knows more about us than we want Him to know. We cannot hide anything from Him because He is everywhere at the same time. God is with us in the day, in the night, even when we call ourselves hiding from Him. Adam and Eve thought they were hiding from God when they ate from the apple and realized they were naked. He was right there waiting for them to confess.

Sometimes, people will say, "he or she died alone." I beg to differ. God was there. I will never forget the time we were about to be on our way to see our father in the hospital after trying to tie up loose ends at home because we knew we were going to spend the entire day and most of the night there. Later, we received a call from the nurse letting us know that our father had passed. In the natural, one would say he died alone. Not so. God was there, the death angel was there, and the heavenly angels were there. God is everywhere because He is the Omnipotent and Omnipresent.

Therefore, we are not to judge anything before the time when the fullness of time shall come, the appointed time, the set time. Those things will bring comfort to our hearts. We can truly say that God sees, hears, and knows all things because He is everywhere at the same time. As we live from day to day, we need to remember that every situation we face has a purpose. God holds us in the palm of His hands and He is directing every situation we face. God controls both the circumstances, the environment, and the thoughts of our hearts. There are no accidents or mistakes with God. His "divine will" will always be done. Even when evil presents itself, God is setting us up for a blessing. There is no way we can fathom the ways in which God works. God works through the good people do and the evil they do. Sometimes we pray for things and only when we receive them do we realize it is not good for us. There are lessons to learn in every facet of our lives.

God being Omnipotent and Omnipresent, His will can be fulfilled in us. When we are in the middle of stressful and worrying situations, or when we are in the midst of difficulty and hardship and things are going topsy turvy, it is in those circumstances that God can be working His purpose out in our lives. It can be financial worries, redundancy, illness, or other uncertainties, as it is today in the natural realm. God's master plan will accomplish all in ways we will not understand. As long as we stay in God's will, forsaking all unrighteousness, we will have peace. There's a song that says, *"I'm leaving all to follow Jesus, I am turning from this world away, Oh I'm stepping upon His promise, And all I have is His today."* Matthew 19:29-30 says, *"And every one that hath forsaken houses, or brethren, or sisters, or father, or mother, or wife, or children, or lands, for my name's sake, shall receive an hundredfold, and shall inherit everlasting life. But many that are first shall be last; and the last shall be first."* God knows when you forsake all, you are totally committed to Him. It is a choice to let go of everything else in order to rely entirely on God. When I sold out to the Lord, I gave up a good boyfriend and an excellent best friend. I did not want anything to hinder me from the kingdom. Was it easy, No! It was a choice. As Hezekiah Walker said in his song, *"My heart is fixed, my mind's made up. No room, no vacancies, I'm all filled up. His spirit lives in me and that's the reason I'm 'souled' out, my mind is made up."* I loved them, but I loved God more. God had more to offer me from earth to glory. Once I gave them up, I kept my mind stayed on God. He gave me the peace which passeth all understanding. He kept my heart and mind.

Peace is greater than money. We can see that through movie stars and musical entertainers. A lot of wealthy, famous, and powerful people would trade everything for just one moment of peace. God's peace is altogether different from the world's peace. *"Peace I leave you, my peace I give to you. Not as the world gives do I give to you. Let not your hearts be troubled, neither let them be afraid" (Joshua 14:27).* The world's peace is always an empty promise and can only bring temporary comfort for a season. When it wears off, sometimes it causes one to go to alcohol and drugs, which becomes habit forming. That is the end of you, and it leads to death.

God's peace is permanent. You can trust Him to keep His Word and heal you everywhere you hurt. God does not ignore your sin, He heals it. God's peace is a different kind of peace from what we find in the world. God offers peace in the midst of chaos. God's peace doesn't change with the circumstances, it is secure in spite of the circumstances. We can trust God's Word. He never contradicts Himself or acts in a way that is out of character. He will never disappoint. *"But when the fullness of time was come" (Galatians 4:4a).* God has a set time and an appointed time to bring circumstances to fruition on our behalf and for our good. God is an on-time God, we just try to make Him work on our time. God's ways and God's thoughts are nowhere near ours. God is sovereign. *"For my thoughts are not your thoughts, neither are your ways, my ways, saith the Lord. For as the heavens are higher than the earth, so are my ways higher than your ways, and my thoughts than your thoughts" (Isaiah 55:8-9).* God's infinite thoughts are for greater than our limited ability to comprehend them. God's ways will not always make sense to us, but we rest in the knowledge, like His Word says, He is always good and therefore everything He does is good. Even when His Word stated that the first shall be last and the last shall be first, God's measurements are different from ours. No one will ever think their status in life will reflect their status in heaven or eternity. We are in this world, so we look at the natural. God is Omnipotent, Omnipresent, and Omniscient. He is a spirit and sees things through the spiritual realm.

With God being everything that the Word says, it is vitally important that we take heed to Paul's question in Romans 8:35, *"Who shall separate us from the love of Christ? Shall tribulation...,"* an affliction that is not taken away, but is sensibly enjoyed in the midst of your affiliation because God is working so many other things out for you? *"These things have I spoken unto you that in me ye might have peace. In this world ye shall have tribulation, but be of good cheer, I have overcome the world" (John 16:33). "I call on the Lord in distress. The Lord answered me and set me in a broad place" (Psalm 118:5).* Hostility and ill treatment from the world are signs that Christ has loved and called us, because the world hates us. Famine, extreme scarcity of food and drought were seen as both punishment and opportunity. Suffering opened the door for repentance and change. Paul, who was deeply in love with Christ, suffered many perils. He faced dangers such as the "sword," a bladed weapon intended for manual cutting or thrusting. James, the brother of Jesus, died when his head was separated from his body, yet the love of God was not separated from him. *"For I am persuaded that neither death, not life, nor angels, nor principalities, nor powers, nor things present nor things to come. Not height, nor depth nor any other creature shall be able to separate us from the love of God which is in Christ Jesus our Lord" (Romans 8:35, 38-39).*

We are going to face various kinds of intense adversity. Nothing can stop Christ's love or separate the body of Christ from His love. Even though situations in our lives make us sad or afraid, God will always love us. He will open up windows for us to see. He is still holding and blessing me. It is God's footprints that are in the sand, not ours.

There are three things that will separate us from the love of God; our own will, sin, and the fascination with world, *"Do not be conformed to this world, but be transformed by the renewing of your minds, so that you may discern what is the will of God, what is good and acceptable and perfect" (Romans 12:2 NRSV).* We are not to conform anymore to the worldly patterns, but be transformed by replacing old, negative thinking or thoughts with new positive Christ-like patterns. When we were of the world, we conformed to fit into someone else's mold and do things the way they have always been done. When we are transformed, our condition, nature, character, and personality will change for the better. If we are not transformed, the Bible says, *"But your iniquities have separated between you and your God, and your sins have hid His face from you that He will not hear" (Isaiah 59:2).* We are to live by the spirit, not the impulses of our flesh.

God does not shelter us from the difficulties of life because we need them to grow spiritually. God allows trials to come, in order that we may learn to depend on Him more. The struggles in this life are not a sign that God has abandoned us, they are hardships in which He works to see us through.

CHAPTER NINE
Stop Worrying and Start Trusting God

Proverbs 3:5-6 says, *"Trust in the Lord with all thine heart, and lean not unto thine own understanding. In all thy ways acknowledge him, and he shall direct thy paths."* In Psalm 34:4, David said he sought the Lord and he answered him and delivered him from all his fears. *"Don't worry about anything; instead, pray about everything. Tell God what you need, and thank him for all he has done. Then you will experience God's peace, which exceeds anything we can understand. His peace will guard your hearts and minds as you live in Christ Jesus"* *(Phillipians 4:6-7 NLT). "Therefore I say unto you, Take no thought for your life, what ye shall eat, or what ye shall drink; nor yet for your body, what ye shall put on. Is not the life more than meat, and the body than raiment? Behold the fowls of the air: for they sow not, neither do they reap, nor gather into barns; yet your heavenly Father feedeth them. Are ye not much better than they? Which of you by taking thought can add one cubit unto his stature? And why take ye thought for raiment? Consider the lilies of the field, how they grow; they toil not, neither do they spin: And yet I say unto you, That even Solomon in all his glory was not arrayed like one of these.*

Wherefore, if God so clothe the grass of the field, which to day is, and to morrow is cast into the oven, shall he not much more clothe you, O ye of little faith? Therefore take no thought, saying, What shall we eat? or, What shall we drink? or, Wherewithal shall we be clothed? (For after all these things do the Gentiles seek:) for your heavenly Father knoweth that ye have need of all these things. But seek ye first the kingdom of God, and his righteousness; and all these things shall be added unto you. Take therefore no thought for the morrow: for the morrow shall take thought for the things of itself. Sufficient unto the day is the evil thereof" (Matthew 6:25-34).

I tell you, people far and near, when you are worrying about something, increase your prayer life. Let the mess in your life become your message. Tell the world your prayer. Life taught you how to trust God and how it drew you closer to God. That is what God really wants. He wants us to lean on him, so that we will be close to Him. He can handle and fix anything and everything we are going through. We have to trust God when we cannot trace Him. Every test, trial, and tribulation supposed to point us to Jesus, so we can draw near to Him and He will draw near to us. That is called having a personal relationship with the Trinity, the Father, the Son, and the Holy Ghost. The three are one, triune.

There is a proverbial saying that goes, "A day of worrying is more exhausting than a day of work." Do not let worrying control your day or your thoughts. Give God full control. He is in control of everything in this universe. Give it to Him submissively, so He will not have to take it by force. God has plans for each one of our lives. All we need to do is say, "Yes, Lord, not my will, but thine will be done." The Bible says to pray without ceasing. Prayer is an essential advantage; it keeps you in a relationship with God. Prayer will transform your life as I said in a previous chapter, in miraculous ways. When we put ourselves in the hands of God, His Word will sustain us. Remember that praying is when we talk to God and reading His Word, is when He talks to us. The two should go hand in hand, daily. Do not let it be one way, "ninety-nine and a half won't do it." That was an extremely popular gospel song back in the seventies. I desire the presence of the Lord, daily, I talk to God, like He is a natural man. Thank God that He says He is our first husband. I respond to Him as my husband because He supplies all my needs. *"But my God shall supply all your needs according to his riches in glory by Christ Jesus" (Philippians 4:19).*

In God's Word, He says, *"Ask, and it shall be given you; seek, and ye shall find; knock, and it shall be opened unto you. For every one that asketh receiveth; and he that seeketh findeth; and to him that knocketh it shall be opened" (Matthew 7:7-8).* Therefore, we should consistently knock at the door of the Lord, so it will always be opened to us. Prayer is a discipline. *"If my people, which are called by my name, shall humble themselves, and pray, and seek my face, and turn from their wicked ways; then will I hear from heaven, and will forgive their sin, and will heal their land" (2 Chronicles 7:14).* Prayer moves God, He said that He will hear from heaven and will (action words) forgive their sin and will (action words) heal their land. When we pray, we ought to pray in Jesus' name. Prayer gives us the authority to pray in His son Jesus' name. There are twenty-four hours in a day, every believer should give God at least one hour of quality time in prayer and reading His Word, then God will lead you from there. I have the mentality that since there are twenty-four hours in a day, ten percent of that is two hours and forty minutes. I try to live from that daily, in praying and reading His Word. It is a big sacrifice, but the benefits are out of this world, which is why I do it with ease by His unction. It is a humbling thing, but the same way He asks for ten percent from our increase to tithe, surely, He wants ten percent of the twenty-four hours He blesses us with daily.

It is easier to trust God, than to worry about things you cannot fix. The following patriarchs had three things in common, faith, hope, and trust in God. The Bible says the Elders obtained a good report, through faith, hope, and trust. Abel offered a pleasing sacrifice. Through trust, Enoch never knew death, Noah built an ark, Abraham left his kinsman, Sara bored a son, Isaac blessed Jacob, Jacob blessed his children, Joseph was warned of famine, Moses led Israel, Israel crossed the sea, Jericho fell down, Rahab spared the spies, Gideon led an army, Samson slew a thousand, Ruth served the Lord, Esther saved the Jews, Elijah called the lightning, David slew a giant, the prophets revealed the word and the Apostles preached Christ, all by faith, hope, and trust. God left all these testimonies on record, so we too can have faith, hope, and trust. We have no need to worry because it only adds to the situation. Satan loves to magnify things. He wants to make you think, you are all alone in this situation and there is no hope for you from God. Satan knows better than anybody, God specializes in things that are impossible. Satan wages attack on the mind because He knows with our mind we serve the Lord. If he can get your mind, he has your soul as well.

The following scriptures will help you build your trust in God when it seems like the victory just will not come or you have the question on the tip of your tongue, "Where is God now?" He is sitting on the right hand of the father because...

1. **God Knows What Will Happen Next.** *"Trust in the Lord with all your heart and lean not on your own understanding, in all your ways submit to Him, and He will make your paths straight"* *(Proverbs 3:5-6 NIV).* Cling to this verse when you are facing uncertainties and difficulties in your life. God sees everything that happens to you. He knows all He has protected you from. God is our protector.

2. **Jesus Never Changes, He is Immutable!** *"Jesus is the same yesterday and today and forever"* *(Hebrews 13:8 ESV).* God is unchanging in His character, will, and His promises. God does not experience emotional change in any way.

3. **Do Not Let News Shake You.** *"He is not afraid of bad news, his heart is firm, trusting in the Lord"* *(Psalm 112:7 ESV).* God is never worried. He gives strength and steadiness to face whatever is ahead when your faith is in Him.

4. **God Is Our Source of Courage.** *"Have I not commanded you? Be strong and courageous. Do not be frightened and do not be dismayed, for the Lord your God is with you wherever you go"* *(Joshua 1:9 ESV).* God is always with you no matter what you face. God does not command you to be courageous in your own strength, but in His.

5. **I Am the Way, the Truth and the Life.** *"Commit thy way unto the Lord, trust also in him and he shall bring it to pass" (Psalm 37:5).* God cannot lie. When He says He will bring it to pass on your behalf, you can believe Him.

6. **God is Omnipresent.** *"Fear thou not, for I am with thee, be not dismayed for I am thy God, I will strengthen thee, yea I will help thee, yea I will hold with the right hand of my righteousness" (Isaiah 41:10).* God does not promise us that walking with Him will keep us from facing difficulties or troubles, but He will be with us in the fire, like He was with the three Hebrew brothers.

7. **God is a Promise Keeper.** *"For the word of the Lord is right, and all his works are done in truth" (Psalm 33:4).* God is a loving and trustworthy God, even in your suffering, He never fails, He keeps His promise.

8. **The Lord is my Shepherd.** *"I am the good shepherd, and know my sheep, and am known of mine" (John 10:14).* There is only one God of the universe who made you, knows what you need and calls you His own.

9. **God Knows What is Good for Us**. *"We know that in all things God works for the good of those who love him, who have been called according to his purpose" (Romans 8:28 NIV).* God can Renew, Revive, and Restore anything that is broken. God always proves

Himself strong whose heart is made perfect toward Him.

10. **God Cares for All Creation.** *"Look at the birds of the air, they do not sow or reap or store away in barns, and yet your heavenly Father feeds them. Are you not much more valuable than they? Can any one of your worries add a single hour to your life" (Matthew 6:26-27 NIV).* God cares for everything He has created, but this particular scripture tells us that He is especially concerned with providing us with what we need.

11. **God is a Safe Place for your Life.** *"Trust in Him at all times, you people pour out your hearts to him, for God's our refuge" (Psalm 62:8 NIV).* You can run to God for security and protection instead of running to things or to other people.

12. **Let Not Your Heart Be Troubled.** *"Let not your hearts be troubled, you believe in God, believe also in me" (John 14:1).* God reminded the disciples and encouraged them that their hearts did not have to be anxious or troubled about believing in Him and His promises, the same way believe in God, believing in Him and His promises, the same way believe in God, believe also in Him, because we are one.

13. **What Happens When the Righteous Cries?** *"This is the confidence we have in approaching God, that if we ask anything according to His will, He hears us" (1 John 5:14 NIV).* If we have a relationship with God

through His son, Jesus, we can trust that He hears our prayers and provides for us in ways that fulfill His will.

14. **We Are to Trust in God, Not in Things.** *"Some trust in chariots and some in horses, but we trust in the name of the Lord, our God" (Psalm 20:7 NIV).* We have no need to trust in anything but God, not in any of the other things that can give deceptive appearance of security, like powerful people, jobs, health, and so on. God is unfailing.

15. **Keep Your Attentiveness on God.** *"Thou wilt keep him in perfect peace, whose mind is stayed on thee, because he trusteth in thee. Trust ye in the Lord for ever, for in the Lord Jehovah is everlasting strength" (Isaiah 26:3-4).* We are blessed to have a trustworthy God knowing we are cared for, that never changes or falters.

16. **When You Are Afraid, Turn to God.** *"When my heart is overwhelmed; Lead me to the rock that is higher than I" (Psalm 61:2b).* David knew that God would care of him, and He will not let His people down.

17. **You Can Trust God for Forgiveness.** *"Many are the woes of the wicked, but the Lord's unfailing love surrounds the one who trusts in Him" (Psalm 32:10 NIV).* You can trust in God because He does not treat or give us what we really deserve.

18. **What to Do with God's Word.** *"We must believe that He is and that He is a rewarder of those who diligently seek Him" (Hebrews 11:6b).* First of all, we must have faith in God, which is the Word, because if we don't have faith, it is impossible to please God. Loving God with all of our heart, soul, and mind means letting go our way of doing things.

19. **We Should Trust What God Has Already Done.** *"And this is the record, that God hath given to us eternal life, and this life is in His Son" (1 John 5:11).* Christ paid for our sins on the cross. We could never achieve what it takes to be in God's presence. Christ did what we could not.

20. **Trusting in God Brings Blessings.** *"I can do all things through Christ which strengtheneth me" (Phillipians 4:13).* The importance of trust and confidence in God, is placing our faith in God. We have access to divine favor, strength, and nourishment that can help us navigate through even the most challenging of circumstances.

CHAPTER TEN
God Told Me, "I AM THINE."

During the separation of my marriage, my life changed financially. The burden of my household had fallen on me, and I had to navigate the steering wheel, so I thought. I began to look at my situation that was present, rather than look at God who plans and schedules the past, present, and the future. If we are not watchful, we will look at how big the problem is, rather than look to God who is much bigger than any of our problems. After reflecting on my problems and situation, I recalled God's promises in His Word: *"Thou wilt keep him in perfect peace, whose mind is stayed on thee" (Isaiah 26:3)*, and *"Yea, though I walk through the valley of the shadow of death, I will fear no evil" (Psalm 23:4)*. These scriptures provided me with comfort, assuring me that I would not remain in that state forever; I would simply pass through it. Remembering that "it came to pass, trouble doesn't last always," and "draw nigh to God and He will draw nigh to you," reminded me that God is a comforter who promises to meet all our needs according to His riches. Trusting in Him, I knew He would lighten the burden of my household and quench the flames of adversity. God assured me, "I am Ishi, your first husband; is there anything too hard for God?" God is the richest husband on this universe. Elon Musk's net worth is $204 billion, Jeff Bezos's is $190 billion, Bernard Arnault's is $182 billion, Mark Zuckerberg's is $170 billion, Bill Gates's is $145 billion, and there are ninety-plus others. They still cannot be compared with God because He created them, the money, and the knowledge to obtain wealth. If you have God, you do not need anything or anyone else. The more I drew closer to God in fasting, praying, and studying His Word, the peace God gave me surpassed all understanding. I know what it means when people say, "Your tests do not come to make you bitter, but they come to make you better."

God is Time, like He told me. God plans our times, schedules our times, and arranges our times when something should take place or happens. I would like to share this poem with you:

Very Nice Definition of TIME
Time is slow when you Wait!
Time is Fast when you are Late!
Time is Deadly when you are Sad!
Time is Short when you are Happy!
Time is Endless when you are in Pain!
Time is Long when you feel Bored!

Author Unknown

Time is determined by our feelings and our psychological conditions and not by clocks. So have a nice time always. I made sure through God and by God that I did not let my present conditions and dark circumstances dictate my appearance and lifestyle. The Bible plainly says, *"We are the light of the world, a city that can bot be hid."* I did not want to appear as a sad sack in sorrow's valley with no hope in God. I would see my other colleagues purchasing their second homes and luxurious cars. I was looking out over the patio in my luxurious apartment on the Mississippi River that I was leasing, but not buying. I told the Lord, with a very low spirit dwelling on the inside, "Lord, I could be much further in life if my husband was here." God spoke out so plainly and loudly, "I am Time. I Make-up for Time." I said, "Yes, Lord," very humbly. I couldn't hurry God. I just had to trust Him and wait. I remember one of the renown pastors in the city said to his audience when I was there visiting, "Waiting time is not wasted time with God." I took that and sealed that in my heart, like I do with God's Word. I think about that, even as of now, when I am met with challenges and defeat.

We look at time naturally through an earthly clock. God is Time. He plans, arranges, and schedules through His timing. One of Lazarus's sisters told Jesus, "Lord, if thou hadst been here, my brother would not have died." She expressed this sentiment three times, seeking solace from Him. Jesus responded, saying, *"Thy brother shall rise again."* Martha, understanding the future resurrection, replied, *"I know that he shall rise again in the resurrection at the last day."* Jesus assured her firmly, *"I am the resurrection, and the life: he that believeth in me, though he were dead, yet shall he live"* (John 11:25). **But when the fullness of time had come.** "When the appointed time arrived, Jesus, with a loud voice, cried, 'Lazarus, come forth' And he that was dead came forth, bound hand and foot with graveclothes: and his face was bound about with a napkin. Jesus said unto them, *'Loose him, and let him go'" (John 11:43-44)*. The onlookers failed to comprehend that Jesus could open the eyes of the blind, and they did not understand that sickness and death could not prevent Lazarus from being healed. They were unaware that **God has a set time, an appointed time, and that the fullness of time had not yet come** for Lazarus to be resurrected or delivered.

Even John, Jesus's beloved disciple, might have had some doubt because John was about to be beheaded for standing up for righteousness. He had heard about the great deeds and miracles Jesus had wrought while he was still in prison. He wanted clarity for himself as well as his disciples that Jesus was the true Messiah, because there were a lot of false prophets declaring they were the real Messiah. John's disciples believed in Jesus, as well as being the only Messiah that was true. John sent his disciples with this message, *"Are thou he that should come, or do we look for another?"* John knew the answer that the real Messiah would give, but he wanted his disciples to hear the truth as well. Jesus told the disciples, go, and shew John again, all the things you have heard and seen. Tell John about the blind who received their sight and the lame who walked. Tell him about the lepers who were cleansed, the deaf who can hear, the dead who were raised up, and the poor who have heard the gospel preached to them. When Jesus heard that John was in prison, Jesus went from Galilee to Decapolis, to Jerusalem, to Judea and from beyond Jordan making disciples of Christ, preaching the gospel, healing all manner of disease among the people. The fullness of time had not come for John, he was beheaded and put on a platter for a young girl that danced before the king celebrating his birthday. The young girl was coached by her mom to ask for such a gift by the king.

Sometimes, our deliverance will not always come the way we expect. **But the fullness of time** is orchestrated and directed by God. God's deliverances come from various facets. We have to say like His son, Jesus said in Luke 22:42, *"Nevertheless, not my will, but thine will be done."* Paul and 276 souls were out on a ship against a tempestuous wind, that was contrary to their traveling. Paul knew the ship would have much hurt and damage and they would be healed toward the quicksands. They all experienced losing "hope." **But when the fullness of time was about to come.** Paul told the people on the ship to be of good cheer, for he believed God, that it shall be even as it was told to him, by the angel of God. *"Except these abide in the ship, ye cannot be saved" (Acts 27:31b).* **But when the full of time had come.** Some swam into the sea to get to dry land. Some were on boards; others were on broken pieces. It came to pass not one soul was lost, that they all escaped to land, their **fullness of time had come.** They met death and was confronted many times during those 14 days out on the sea. God holds the keys to death and hell. Oh, how their faith was tested and challenged. That is why it is so comforting and rewarding to have a relationship with the Trinity. In the midst of it all, Paul had a relationship even though he faced death many times out on the sea, and he was headed to court for righteousness' sake. Paul had already gone from judgement hall to judgement hall. Paul had to go before governors and kings. He testified before Governor Festus, Governor Felix, and King Agrippa, that he had not done anything illegal, but he was being tried because of his belief in the resurrection of the dead. God wanted Paul to testify to the Roman Emperor, Caesar too, so he could hear about Jesus. Paul received the victory in the end, because we are overcomers, and we are more than conquerors. Like all believers, even Jesus, we have, and we will face many challenges, while on the Lord's assignment. It is all for God's glory, behind our story.

Whatever betides us, our testimony is to point someone to Jesus. Jesus is the atonement for our sins, the propitiation for our sins and the ransom sacrifice for sins. This whole universe should be centered following God's Son, obeying His commandments, and fulfilling the purpose He has destined for us. Timing is everything to God, we do not know the day not the hour, that God is going to call us home. That is why we need to work our soul, salvation with fear, and trembling. We do not want the Lord to call us, and our work is undone. My question to you, reader, since you have been born and lived on this earth, what have you done with your time for God. Have you used your time wisely for God, or are you pleasing others? God is a jealous God. I would like to give you some scriptures on God being jealous. *"I am the Lord thy God, which have brought thee out of the land of Egypt, out of the house of bondage. Thou shalt have no other gods before me"* (Exodus 20:2-3). *"Thou shalt not bow down thyself to them, nor serve them, for I the Lord thy God am a jealous God"* (Exodus 20:5a). *"For thou shalt worship no other god, for the Lord whose name is Jealous, is a Jealous God"* (Exodus 34:14). God does not want others to take what is rightfully His. God is a giving God, because He gave His very best, when He gave His "only begotten son" and God is a sharing God. He has given man dominion over everything on this earth. But one thing that God makes plain over in Isaiah. *"I am the Lord that is my name, and my glory will I not give to another, neither my praise to graven images" (Isaiah 42:8).* God is also jealous when He doesn't have a relationship with us. He wants us to be on speaking terms with Him. Speaking terms are when you talk to Him daily in prayer and He will talk to you, concerning your problems or situations, your happiness or encouragement through reading the Bible daily, that is the kind of relationship He wants instead of being jealous. Just like you want your spouse to communicate or affirm you daily, that is exactly what God wants. *"For the Lord thy God is a consuming fire, even a jealous God. But if from thence thou shalt seek the Lord thy God, thou shalt find him, if thou seek him with all thy heart and with all thy soul" "And Joshua said unto the people, Ye cannot serve the Lord: for he is an holy God; he is a jealous God; he will not forgive your transgressions nor your sins. If ye forsake the Lord, and serve strange gods, then he will turn and do you hurt, and consume you, after that he hath done you good" (Joshua 24:19-20).* Our Times should be in God's hands, and He should always be first place, considering every aspect of our lives and pointing to His Son, Jesus. The final scripture on the jealousy of God is: *"He that loveth father or mother more than me is not worthy of me, and he that loveth son or daughter more than me is not worthy of me" (Matthew 10:37).* God has it in His Word how strong His jealously is concerning us. It is stronger than a man over his wife or woman. God is very possessive of us.

CHAPTER ELEVEN
Heed to God's Calling and Warning

W e as disciples of Christ, believers of Christ, followers of Christ and new converts, must take heed, to the one who set us free out of bondage. When God speaks audibly or to our hearts, we need to first, pay attention, be concerned, consider everything He says and how He says it. Then take an interest, note everything he says in writing, observe and give credence to it. You should also regard it with your heart. God also uses prophets, preachers, and teachers, to give you messages. Sometimes, He will speak to you from someone that is not affiliated with the church. God uses whomever He wants. In the Bible, He used a rooster and a donkey to declare a message. We must have an ear to hear and heed the warning. Sometimes, you can be on the wrong path, following the wrong people, listening to the wrong people, traveling with the wrong people, or even eating with the wrong people. God is not concerned "about those people who are relatives." He said, *"Wherefore come out from among them, and be ye separate, saith the Lord, and touch not the unclean thing; and I will receive you"* (2 Corinthians 6:17). *"Can two walk together, except they be agreed?"* (Amos 3:3) *"And have no fellowship with the unfruitful works of darkness, but rather reprove them" (Ephesians 5:11). "Be ye not unequally yoked together with unbelievers, for what fellowship hath righteousness with unrighteousness? and what communion hath light with darkness?" (2 Corinthians 6:14)* We are not to be bound or have close ties with the unbeliever. Believers can and should relate to unbeliever's situations, but we must never emulate or mirror their lifestyles or ungodly habits. Our relationship with God will cause us to put a knife at our throat at the devil's dainties. *"And put a knife to thy throat, if thou be a man given to appetite. Be not desirous of his dainties: for they are deceitful meat" (Proverbs 23:2-3).* These are warnings we want to take heed to. Warning comes before destruction.

I am reminded of Lot's wife in the Bible. Lot is Abraham's nephew, who lived in Sodom with his family. God sent two angels to warn Lot's wife and two daughters, to flee from the city before God destroys it. The angels told them to "Escape for your life! Do not look behind you and do not stay anywhere in the valley, escape to the mountains, or you will be swept away." Lot and his daughters took heed to the warning, but his wife did not. She looked back, and immediately turned into a pillar of salt. She valued what was behind her more than obeying God in heeding the warning. *"And Jesus said unto him, No man, having put his hand to the plough, and looking back, is fit for the kingdom of God" (Luke 9:62).* Jesus wants us to look straight ahead and leave this old life behind. Press toward the mark for the prize of the high calling of God in Christ Jesus. The song says, "I'm leaving all to follow Jesus." Heed the Warning! Heed the Warning! It is very important that we do. It can be a life-or-death call. Lot's daughters knew to obey the angels of God, this is an individual matter. We all will have to stand before God and give an account of everything that God has on our record. *"The Lord shall count, when he writeth up the people"* (Psalm 87:6a).

God told Abraham to take his only son, the one that was born at his old age, and the one he truly loved, and to carry him to the land of Moriah and offer him as a burnt offering. Abraham began to comply, tied Isaac to the altar and pulled out his knife. God sent a ram from the bush for Abraham to sacrifice. God tested Abraham. Abraham heeded the call, even though it took Abraham and Sarah twenty-five years before Sarah could have Isaac. He was willing to obey God, and demonstrate his faith, since Abraham heeded the calling. God told Abraham that he will be the father of many nations. God also told Abraham that he will make his descendants as numerous as the stars in the sky and when he arrived in Israel, God told him that He will give him the land for his descendants.

Even in the beginning, Adam and Eve did not heed the warning from God. They were given the ability and responsibility to decide whether to heed God's command or choose to obey Him. One thing I can truly say is that God is a gentleman. He is not going to force righteousness on you. It has to be your own choice. If you disobey God, He will bring disaster in your life, incurable diseases, and fevers that will make you blind and cause your life to waste away. *"And if ye will not for all this hearken unto me, but walk contrary unto me. Then I will walk contrary unto you also in fury, and I, even I, will chastise you seven times for your sins"* (Leviticus 21:27-28). God told Adam and Eve they could eat from any tree in the garden except the tree of the knowledge of good and evil. God told them if they would do otherwise, they would surely die. After they ate from the tree of knowledge, they immediately recognized their sin. God cursed the serpent that beguiled them and the ground. Eve suffered through childbirth and Adam had to work by the sweat of his brow. They were forever banished from the Garden of Eden because God closed it from them permanently, and that is when sin entered the earth. They had two sons, Cain and Abel. Out of jealousy, Cain killed his brother, Abel. Cain was the first murderer and the first human born according to the book of Genesis. Abel offered God a pleasing sacrifice, which was the first and best from his flock. Cain did not give God his first nor his best, and this was displeasing to God.

God told Noah to warn the people that they must repent and be baptized, or they would be destroyed by floods. The people refused to heed the warning and became angry at Noah and wanted to kill him. They could not kill Noah, because God had a plan for Noah and his family which consisted of his wife, their three sons and their wives. God told Noah to build an ark, because He was going to destroy the earth by flood. The people laughed at Noah and thought he was crazy for building an ark, and never thought it would rain. If God says it, that settles it. God told Noah what to carry on the ark and gave him the measurements of the ark to build. God told Noah that in seven days He would send rain on the earth. He told him that it would rain for forty days and forty nights. Every living creature that was left on earth was destroyed, along with all the people because they did not heed the warning. The earth was flooded for 150 days and Noah, his family, and all the animals stayed in the ark for 371 days. Everything was provided for them by Noah, led by God's directions and calling. God made a covenant with Noah, that he will never the destroy the earth or lives again by flood. A rainbow will always be a sign for the covenant He made with Noah and every living creature. It behooves each of us to heed God's warning immediately.

Moses did not take heed to God's instruction. The children of Israel were crying to Moses for water. Moses went to God and God gave him specific instructions to follow. God told Moses to gather all the Israelites in front of the rock and Aaron, thy brother, and speak ye unto the rock before their eyes and it shall bring forth water out of the rock. Moses was frustrated with the Israelites and called them Rebels and exclaimed, "Should I give you water out of this rock?" Moses lifted up his hand, with his rod in it and smote the rock twice, and the water came out abundantly and the congregation and beasts did drink. In Numbers Chapter 20, Moses was instructed by God to speak to the rock, but he disobeyed by striking the rock instead of speaking to it. God told Moses that because of his disobedience, He will not bring the children of Israel to the Promised Land. Moses was barred from the Promised Land for not taking heed.

Jonah also did not take heed to God's calling. God called Jonah to go to Nineveh, a wicked city and prophesy to them if they did not stop their evil doings and wicked ways. He was going to overturn the city. Jonah rebelled against God and went in the opposite direction of Nineveh. God sent a storm to stop Jonah. The boat that Jonah was on threw Jonah overboard. God prepared a big fish to swallow up Jonah. Jonah began to pray and repent in the fish's belly. God let the fish spit him up on the shore near Ninevah. God called Jonah the second time to preach to Ninevah. He heeded the call this time and the whole city repented, and Jonah wanted Ninevah to be destroyed by God, because when the children of Israel crossed the Red Sea, coming out of Egypt, Ninevah went against them, and Jonah did not forget about what happened to his ancestors. When things like that happen in our lives, we are human, and it hurts. Our flesh would like to fight back when we have the upper hand. We have to turn it over to God. He will fix it and fight for us. God is our battleax. We are not to take up for ourselves, which is so easy to do. We have to let go and let God. That way, we will not have to suffer like Jonah did. The Bible says when the big fish spat him out, he took a three-day journey and made it in one day, because of God's wrath. No battle is ever ours; it belongs to God. God has called us to be holy, for He is holy. We are transformed by the renewing of our minds. A widow woman and Elijah both had to heed to God's calling and warning. God had told Elijah to go to Zarephath because He had commanded a widow woman to sustain or feed him. He had to have faith in God to believe a widow woman would sustain him. That can be a little humiliating to ask a strange woman for food. When Elijah met her, he just started out by asking for a little water first. When his courage had built up, he then asked for a morsel of bread. The widow woman told Elijah that she did not have cake, but a handful of meal in a barrel and a little oil in a cruse. The woman said, "Behold, I am gathering two sticks, that I may go in and dress it for me and my son, that we may eat it and die." Elijah told the discouraged widow woman to go on and do as she said she would do. He then told her to make him a little cake first and bring it to him, and afterward to make a cake for her and her son. He told her that God said her barrel of meal shall not lack, neither shall the cruse of oil be empty, until the day that the Lord sends rain upon the earth. Everything Elijah told her came to pass. It took faith, hope, trust, and belief for each of them to believe. Elijah had to heed the call from God, in order to ask a widow woman to do such. The widow woman had to trust and believe God to put a stranger before her and her son. A man should be able to take care of himself and provide for the widow woman and her son. Our ways and thoughts are not like God. We have to trust Him when He gives a command, a warning or a call. Before Elijah left, the widow woman's son got sick, and he revived him back to life and prayed for him. The woman said to Elijah that she knew now thou art a man of God and that the Word of the Lord in thy mouth is true. For some people, it is hard for them to believe, even after seeing evidence. It took two miracles for her to witness until all doubt was eradicated.

Rahab was a harlot, but she had sense enough to heed to God's warning and calling. God has no respecter of person when it comes to God's calling and warning. Two of the Israelites' spies had come to spy out the land of Jericho. The king of Jericho was informed of their presence and was told they stopped at Rahab, the harlot's house because that is where men would lodge. Rahab hid the two spies and told the King's men they were last seen going out the gate and told the men to pursue after them quickly and ye will overtake them. Rahab had actually brought the two spies of Israel, to the top of the roof of her roof of her house and hid them with the stalks of flax. Rahab was a harlot, but she had a calling on her life and she walked in it for the people of God. She told the two spies, *"I know that the Lord hath given you the land, and that your terror is fallen upon us, and that all the inhabitants of the land faint because of you. For we have heard how the Lord dried up the water of the Red Sea for you, when ye came out of Egypt; and what ye did unto the two kings of the Amorites, that were on the other side Jordan, Sihon and Og, whom ye utterly destroyed. And as soon as we had heard these things, our hearts did melt, neither did there remain any more courage in any man, because of you: for the Lord your God, he is God in heaven above, and in earth beneath" (Joshua 2:9-11).* Look at this harlot. Rahab, confessing out of her own mouth, who God is. She has no doubt, who God is and what God can do. She has already been persuaded to become one of them, a disciple of God. Rahab told the spies, *"Now therefore, I pray you, swear unto me by the Lord, since I have shewed you kindness, that ye will also shew kindness unto my father's house, and give me a true token: And that ye will save alive my father, and my mother, and my brethren, and my sisters, and all that they have, and deliver our lives from death"* (Joshua 2:12-13).

The two spies told Rahab, the harlot, "If you will save our lives, we will save yours." They assured Rahab that when they returned to Jericho and the Lord gave them the land, they would deal kindly and truly with her. After Rahab let them down from the roof, she told them to hide in the mountains for three days before going on their way. They swore that they would keep the oath when they returned to Jericho, instructing her to put and tie the line of scarlet thread in the window through which she let them down and to bring her family and entire household into her house. The spies warned her that if anyone went out of the doors of the house, his blood would be upon his head, but all who remained inside would be under their protection. The spies also cautioned Rahab that if she uttered their business, the oath would be void and null. The spies then left and did everything Rahab told them to do, and when they returned to Joshua, they said, *"Truly the Lord hath delivered into our hands all the land; for even all the inhabitants of the country do faint because of us" (Joshua 2:24).* The Lord had given Joshua the city where Rahab lived. Josua told the two men that had spied out the city, to go to Rahab's house and bring her and all her household out. They all joined up with Israel. They burnt the city with fire and all that was in the city, except the silver, gold, vessels of brass and iron. They put all those into the treasury of the house of the Lord. Joshua saved Rahab, the harlot alive, and her father's household and all that she had, the Bible says Rahab dwelleth in Israel even unto to this day, because she kept her word and her calling and hid the messengers that Joshua sent to spy out Jericho.

Caleb took heed to God's calling along with Joshua. Their faith increased when they saw that God had brought them out of Egypt with the Israelites through the Red Sea into the wilderness. They were chosen by Moses along with the ten other men to explore the Promised Land and give a full report to Moses and all the people. The twelve men had gone to explore Canaan, which flows with milk and honey. They had reported that and even brought back fruit. Ten out of the twelve men said that the people who lived there were very powerful, the cities were fortified and very large. They reported that the Anakites, who were giants, dwelt there along with their descendants. The Israelites were afraid after hearing that. Caleb, who was willing to answer God's calling, had a different outlook and attitude from the other spies. Caleb silenced the people before Moses and said, *"We should go up and take possession of the land, for we can certainly do it" (Numbers 13:30).* The people complained that they could not go up to conquer Canaan. Caleb and Joshua responded strongly to the children of Israel, the land they passed through and explored is exceedingly good. They told the children of Israel, if the Lord is pleased, then the Lord will lead them to Canaan that flows with milk and honey and give them Canaan. Caleb and Joshua told them not to be afraid of the people, because the Lord was with them, the children of Israel. God judged the children of Israel, because they had no faith, so He made them wait 40 years before they entered Canaan. God told them that every person 50 years old or older would die in the wilderness and would not see the Promised Land except Caleb and Joshua, because they had a different spirit and followed the Lord wholeheartedly.

Moses had died 40 years later. Joshua led the people to the Promised land as the Bible states it. Caleb received an inheritance in the Promised Land in his old age. From Joshua and Caleb experiences, we are to stand for God, even when others will not. God will bless us with unforeseen blessings that we cannot imagine or think. Caleb spied out the land at 40 years old, but he did not possess any of it until he was 85 years old. I love the words of Caleb at his old age of 85. Caleb said, *"Here I am today, 85 years old. I am still as strong today as the day Moses sent me out; I was 40 years old then. You yourself heard then that the Anakites were there and their cities were large and fortified, but with the Lord's help, I will drive them out just as he said"* (Joshua 14:10-12).

Nehemiah had an exceptional calling on his life and he heeded the calling with many, many distractions. The people made fun of the work he was doing for the Lord and even made jokes. That is why, when you are working for the Lord, you must stay focused and know that God called you, come what may. While things are going well with you, put on spiritual strength, fasting the more, studying God's Word the more, praying the more, and lying out before God. If you do all the above, you will be able to stand the storm, go through without being bitter, your light will shine so, until people will testify for you.

Just as I mentioned earlier, when my colleague said I looked as if I didn't go through anything, it was during one of the darkest moments of my life. Nobody knew the trouble I had seen. It was at that time, that God was carrying me through the sand. I did not have the strength to carry my burden and teach 180 students a day. But God! He was under the load. God covered me and made my face like a flint. God kept a smile on my face, but down on the inside, I voiced the words of this song, "If the Lord don't help me, I can't stand the storm. If I couldn't say a word, I'll just wave my hand." That is why it is very essential to read God's Word daily so it can encourage you along the way. Nehemiah's story voices the sentiments of one of my life's stories.

Nehemiah received a message from certain men of Judah, telling him the wall of Jerusalem is broken down and the gates are burned with fire. After hearing this, Nehemiah sat down and wept and mourned certain days, fasted, and prayed before God. Nehemiah had a sad countenance that the king was not used to seeing. He questioned Nehemiah about his countenance and Nehemiah told him why. The king immediately asked him what his request was. Look at God working for Nehemiah. Nehemiah asked the king if he would send him to Judah, that he may rebuild. The king asked him how long he would need and will he return. Nehemiah gave him a time frame. The king gave Nehemiah letters to give to the various governors along the way to support him. He had great support except for two big officials who were grieved by his coming and rebuilding Jerusalem's walls and gates. Nehemiah was led by the Lord every step of the way. He told the men that were with him his plans and they immediately responded, "Let us rise up and build." The two men that were grieved about their coming, laughed them to scorn, and questioned them. Nehemiah knew who he was and whose he was. He answered with confidence to the enemy, *"The God of heaven, he will prosper us, therefore we his servants will arise and build, but ye have no portion, nor right, nor memorial in Jerusalem" (Nehemiah 2:20b)*. Nehemiah had hundreds of men to help him rebuild. If God is for you, who can be against you! Sanballot and Tobiah were still mocking them and shouting out threats. Tobiah said a fox can go up the gate and break down the stone. Nehemiah kept on praying and building. One thing that is very important, is that we have to know that if God called you, do not look at the circumstance. The outlook will look gloomy, but the uplook is glorious. We have to keep our mind on God, and he will keep us in perfect peace.

Sanballot, Tobiah, and other great men conspired to come and fight against Jerusalem and to hinder the work of the Lord. No weapon formed me shall prosper. It might form, but it will come to nought. They really thought they had a plan; the devil had tricked their minds. They really thought they would not be recognized, until they came in the midst of them to kill them and stop the work of the Lord. God gave Nehemiah to set up a watch day and night. *"Be not ye afraid of them: remember the Lord, which is great and terrible, and fight for your brethren, your sons, and your daughters, your wives, and your houses. And it came to pass, when our enemies heard that it was known unto us, and God had brought their counsel to nought, that we returned all of us to the wall, everyone unto his work"* *(Nehemiah 4:14b-15).* Nehemiah had all the rulers backing Judah. Everyone kept on building and working with their swords girded by their sides. He also had a group of men, who just watched and guarded with their spears, shields, bows, and breastplates. Nehemiah kept the trumpeters near him so they could alert the people when the enemy would attack. Nehemiah wore many hats, but God equipped him for the task. Wherever God guides, He will provide. Nehemiah was able to build the wall and finished it in 52 days. Even the enemies witnessed and knew that the work was wrought of God. Various things we go through, and experiences are for the sake of Christ. It is to report unbelievers to Jesus. Unbelievers need to know, there is only one true and living God. The only way we can get to heaven is to go through his son, Jesus. If you try to come through anyone or anything else, you come as a thief in the night. The way to Heaven is only through Jesus Christ, and Jesus Christ alone. He does not show the way, He is the way! Jesus is the way, the truth, and the life. Nehemiah concluded after receiving the victory, "I'm doing a great work, and I cannot come down." God had a great calling on Nehemiah's life. It took much love for God and the Gospel of Christ, to heed the calling. That is why, when things are going well with you, get rooted and grounded in God's Word. So, you can have something to refer to when things are black and bleak in your life. You can always give back and quote God's Word to Him and it will not go void. You can begin like this, "But God, You said in Your Word in 1 Peter 5:7 for us to cast all our cares upon You, and You will care for us." Then we can look for God to sustain us and never permit us to be moved. We must humble ourselves under God's mighty hand and let Him exalt us at exactly the right time. God is trustworthy to handle our worries and anxieties in the way that is best for us. Nehemiah trusted Him in everything.

Hosea had a great command and calling from God. In this case, he had to love God with all his heart and trust Him, regardless of what people thought or might have said to him about the calling God had given him. First of all, we need to establish that the name Hosea, means help, deliverance, and salvation. God told Hosea to marry a wife of whoredoms and have children of whoredoms. The book of Hosea does not discuss how he felt behind a command from God like that. We know that Hosea obeyed God. Sometimes the calling on our lives is not understandable. Yet we are called to live by faith, which sometimes includes taking risks that do not make sense. We must trust God and obey Him always.

Hosea married Gomer; a woman he knew committed adultery. Marriage according to God was instituted to be a lifelong promise between a man and a woman; to be faithful, and to help one another. Hosea's marriage would serve as a symbol for the relationship between God and His people. Gomer gave birth to three children, whose names reflected the state of the nation, sad. Israel was in a sad state of condition. The first child was named Jezreel, which means I will punish the house of Jehu for the blood of Jezreel and God will put an end to the kingdom's house of Israel. The second child was named, Lo-Ruhamah, because God would show no mercy to Israel. The third child was named Lo-Ammi, Israel is not my people. Finally, Gomer leaves Hosea and commits adultery, but eventually Hosea buys her back, taking her into his home and forgives her. Isn't that something, having to buy something that is already yours? This symbolizes God buying

Israel back and forgiving her sins. Israel had turned to other gods. They separated themselves from the only true and living God. God used Hosea's own life as a symbol for marrying Gomer, who would be unfaithful to him. The stories of the covenant relationships were violated and then restored back to God. *"If my people, which are called by my name, shall humble themselves and pray and seek my face, and turn from their wicked ways, then will I hear from heaven, and will forgive their sin, and will heal their land" (2 Chronicles 7:14).*

David's command and warning was different from other patriarchs. David wanted to build God a temple. God had been really good to David, after succeeding the kingship of King Saul. God had given David rest from all of his enemies. David had a conversation with Nathan, the prophet, about how he dwells in a house of cedar, but the ark of God dwells in a tent. Nathan told David to do everything that was in his heart. Nathan thought that it was a good idea, but it was not a God idea. God told Nathan to go and tell David that He would give him rest from all his enemies, and once his days had been fulfilled, He will raise up his offspring after him, that He would build the temple and He will establish the throne of his kingdom forever.

God put David in place to be a great king and a great warrior. These were his callings. God gave David the power to destroy many nations, because He did not want those nations to dwell among the Promised Land. God felt like they would pollute the true worship of God if they lived in the Promised Land and that the Israelites would eventually adopt their religion even though they saw all the signs and wonders that God wrought in Egypt. They even saw how God delivered them out of Pharoah's hand. God knew the Israelites would mix their religion with theirs. God made sure these nations would be put under the subjection by the hand of David. God approved of David shedding blood with his hand. David was definitely in the will of God; it was not his flesh that gave him those victories and delivered him. David knew it was the Sovereign God. As long as David and the Israelites obeyed God, they did not have to worry about invasion from other nations.

David explained to the Israelites why he couldn't build the temple but assured them he had made preparations to build a house of rest for the ark of the covenant of the Lord and for God's footstool. David told them that God had said, *"You are a man of war and have shed much blood."* David told them that God had chosen Solomon, his son, to build the house and courts for God. God has chosen him to be his son and he will be the father and establish his kingdom forever if he keeps his commandments as he is doing today. Near the end of David's life, David made a statement, that Solomon was young and inexperienced, and God's house must be exceedingly magnificent of fame and glory throughout all nations. So, David provided materials in great, great quantity before his death. Again, I would like to reiterate that David had not sinned because of the blood on his hands, but God was making a point that the temple must be built by those who have not shed blood, and then the temple of God will be in the people of God with the spirit of God and those are the "redeemed."

Before I close out with the calling and warning of David, I would like to express that David had great sin in his life. God still left on record that David was a man after his own heart. David sinned with Bathsheba and made her pregnant. David even had her husband killed, even though he was out fighting for David to cover Bathsheba's pregnancy by him. The Bible says for us to keep a repentance of heart, and this is what we should pray to God when we have sinned willfully and with commission. *"Have mercy on me, O God, according to your unfailing love; according to your great compassion blot out my transgressions. Wash away all my iniquity and cleanse me from my sin. For I know my transgressions, and my sin is always before me. Against you, you only, have I sinned and done what is evil in your sight; so, you are right in your verdict and justified when you judge. Surely I was sinful at birth, sinful from the time my mother conceived me. Yet you desired faithfulness even in the womb; you taught me wisdom in that secret place. Cleanse me with hyssop, and I will be clean; wash me, and I will be whiter than snow. Let me hear joy and gladness; let the bones you have crushed rejoice. Hide your face from my sins and blot out all my iniquity. Create in me a pure heart, O God, and renew a steadfast spirit within me. Do not cast me from your presence or take your Holy Spirit from me. Restore to me the joy of your salvation and grant me a willing spirit, to sustain me. Then I will teach transgressors your ways, so that sinners will turn back to you. Deliver me from the guilt of bloodshed, O God, you who are God my Savior, and my tongue will sing of your righteousness. Open my lips, Lord, and my mouth will declare your praise. You do not delight in sacrifice, or I would bring it; you do not take pleasure in burnt offerings. My sacrifice, O God, is a broken spirit; a broken and contrite heart you, God, will not despise"* (Psalms 51:1-17).

Solomon, David's son had a calling and a warning on his life. God appeared to Solomon in a dream by night, and God asked Solomon, what He should give thee. Solomon did not ask for riches or the neck of his enemies. He told God to give him

WISDOM! David had already instilled in Solomon's heart an appreciation of wisdom. Even as disciples of Christ, we are in dire need for God's wisdom as Solomon who ran an empire. We should continually ask God for wisdom to navigate through this walk with God as his disciples.

David told Solomon to take courage and be a man, observe the requirements of the Lord your God, and follow all His ways. He told them to keep the decrees, commands, regulations, and laws written in the Law of Moses, so that he would be successful in all that he does and wherever he goes. Solomon was disobedient. He began to marry other women; that turned him away from God and Solomon started worshipping their gods. God had turned the kingdom away from Solomon and gave it to one of his servants. Solomon had a weakness for foreign women. He married seven hundred women and had another three hundred concubines. Many of them came from the nations God prohibited the Israelites from marrying because God knew they would lead the Israelites to worship other gods.

Solomon had everything going for him and none of the decisions he made early on were malicious or ill-intended. But slowly as he went through life, not watching and praying, his heart became insensitive. The beautiful gift that God blessed him with, wisdom, became an instrument for self-service and exaltation. God hates a proud spirit. Solomon said these words, *"But if a man live many years, and rejoice in them all; yet let him remember the days of darkness; for they shall be many. All that cometh is vanity. Rejoice, O young man, in thy youth; and let thy heart cheer thee in the days of thy youth, and walk in the ways of thine heart, and in the sight of thine eyes: but know thou, that for all these things God will bring thee into judgment. Therefore remove sorrow from thy heart, and put away evil from thy flesh: for childhood and youth are vanity"* (Ecclesiastes 11:8-10). *"Vanity of vanities, saith the preacher; all is vanity. And moreover, because the preacher was wise, he still taught the people knowledge; yea, he gave good heed, and sought out, and set in order many proverbs. The preacher sought to find out acceptable words: and that which was written was upright, even words of truth. The words of the wise are as goads, and as nails fastened by the masters of assemblies, which are given from one shepherd. And further, by these, my son, be admonished: of making many books there is no end; and much study is a weariness of the flesh. Let us hear the conclusion of the whole matter: Fear God, and keep his commandments: for this is the whole duty of man. For God shall bring every work into judgment, with every secret thing, whether it be good, or whether it be evil"* (Ecclesiastes 12:8-14).

One thing we want to learn from God's calling and warning is to not get distracted and stay focused on the things of God. He finished his life surrounded by hundreds of beautiful women, untold riches and every type of pleasure that a person could ever desire. Solomon died a shell of a man, empty. It was the lust of the eyes, the lust of the flesh, and the pride of life, which made the temple being taken from him and his soul to be lost. He was so caught up in the above three, he never said what his father, David said, when he got out of the will of God. *"Create in me a clean heart, O God; and renew a right spirit within me. Cast me not away from thy presence; and take not thy holy spirit from me. Restore unto me the joy of thy salvation; and uphold me with thy free spirit"* (Psalm 51: 10-12).

God called Jeremiah to bring a word from God to the people of Israel. Jeremiah was very reluctant to answer the call. God reassured Jeremiah and told him not to be afraid, for He will be with him and put His Word in his mouth. Jeremiah said he was just a child. The same way God used a donkey, a rooster, and other things to carry out His Word, He can use a child as well. Solomon was a child, Josiah was a child, and Jeremiah was a child. The Bible says in Isaiah, "...and a little shall lead them." Despite his initial reluctances, Jeremiah ultimately accepted his divine calling and become one of the most significant prophets in the biblical tradition.

God said, *"Before I formed you in the womb, I knew you, before you were born, I sanctified you and I ordered you a prophet to the nations" (Jeremiah 1:5).* God will always equip us when He calls us. Jeremiah transformed from a hesitant youth to a confident prophet. That should encourage us to find strength, purpose, and identity in the vision that God has for our lives. The Bible lets us know that God touched Isaiah's lips to cleanse them. Jeremiah had reluctant lips and God touched them to excite them. God touched Ezekial's lips for encouragement.

Every believer has a calling on their life. Every believer is sanctioned by God for a specific ministry. We were brought into this world to complete our ministry. Every believer is equipped by God for his or her ministry. Every believer will give an account for the performance of their ministry. Jeremiah had a difficult ministry and was persecuted severely for doing the will of God and was beaten and arrested. Jeremiah experienced being an instrument at the hands of the officials in the temple. Jeremiah cried out that he felt deceived by God. He prophesied to the people and they treated him poorly. He was a laughingstock who was mocked constantly by everyone. His frustration surfaced that he had to constantly bring himself to turn away from God's Word, even though his friends were waiting for him to fail. They wanted to pronounce him as a false prophet. Jeremiah did get discouraged along the way in carrying out his ministry. We need to arm ourselves likewise. Jeremiah provides an important example to all of us in ministry, that serving God is not always easy. Jeremiah shows us that even though we might face great difficulty, we can bring our concern to the Lord, standing on His promises and trusting Him to bring about justice in God's own time.

Even though Jeremiah said he will not make mention of God, nor His prophecies, nor will he speak any more in His name, Jeremiah said His Word was in his heart as a burning fire shut up in his bones. He said he was weary with forbearing and could not stay. *"But the Lord is with me as a terrible one, therefore my persecutors shall stumble and they shall not prevail" (Jeremiah 20:11a).*

Joel was a patriarch that was called to make an announcement to Judah after being invaded with a severe drought and a plague of locusts. The locusts caused starvation for the animals and people. The only thing the children of Israel had to do was lament and repent. God wanted the priests and religious leaders to proclaim the importance of seeking God with a broken heart and a contrite spirit. If all the people would take heed to Joel's announcement, God will reverse the Day of the Lord, turning it from judgement into salvation. He said He will defeat the drought and the invading locusts by turning them away. He would restore the land and make it abundant and full of life once again. They will also be accessible to God's divine presence. When we delight ourselves in fasting, weeping, and mourning, then God delights Himself in us. It is so easy for us to return back to God. First of all, He is married to us. God does not ever leave, we leave Him. God is very gracious and compassionate. He is slow to anger and has an abundance of mercy to give to us. *"But the mercy of the Lord is from everlasting upon them that fear him, and his righteousness unto children's children" (Psalm 103:17).* Joel also prophesied that God's people would be filled with visions, dreams, and the power of the Spirit. When they turn from their wicked ways, God said that they will recover all and He will restore the years that the locust hath eaten, the cankerworm, the caterpillar, and the palmerworm. Judah shall eat in plenty and be satisfied, praising the name of the Lord, that hath dealt wondrously with them and they will never be ashamed. God gave them corn, wine, and oil, and they were forever satisfied. All the trees bore their fruit and yielded much. Everyone knew they had repented and quit their wicked ways. God was their stay. God is the same yesterday, today, and forevermore. The same God back then is the same God right now. *"Brethren, my heart's desire and prayer to God for Israel is, that they might be saved" (Romans 10:1).*

Habakkuk shows us a picture of people who are proud, but God humbled them, while the righteous lived by their faith in God. Sometimes, it reminds us that while God may seem silent and uninvolved in our welfare and wellbeing, He is really right there carrying us through our troubles and worries. If you would be true to yourself, you know and I know that without God we can do nothing. He seems distant to us, because He does not move or work things out, the way we feel He should do or in a timely manner that we expect Him to. As believers, God is present and involved in every step of our lives. God is so sovereign until His ways and timings are past understanding or finding out. Habakkuk encourages us as believers to wait on the Lord, expecting that He will indeed work out all things for our good, it might not feel good, but it is for our good. God knows what is best for us regardless of how black, bleak, and gloomy the situation might be. Sometimes the walls are so thick, and you feel nothing can bring it down. Remember, man's extremities are God's opportunities. Yes, we know God can fix everthing that is broken, "Right Now!" God can right every wrong, "Right Now!" He can make the crooked straight, "Right Now!" He Can Do Anything but Fail, "Right Now!" God wants to teach us patience and increase our faith in Him. Everything we go through is for us to draw close to God, take our yoke and learn of Him, trust Him, and never doubt Him. *"But let patience have her perfect work, that ye may be perfect and entire, wanting for nothing" (James 1:4).* The Lord told Habakkuk, *"...Write the vision, and make it plain upon tables, that he may run that readeth it. For the vision is yet for an appointed time, but at the end it shall speak, and not lie: though it tarry, wait for it; because it will surely come, it will not tarry" (Habakkuk 2:3-4).*

Timing from Bad to Good Through God's Timing

Saul was on the road to Damascus to seek out and arrest followers of Jesus, as mandated by the High Priest, so they would become prisoners to be executed in Jerusalem. *"And as he journeyed, he came near Damascus: and suddenly there shined round about him a light from heaven: and he fell to the earth, and heard a voice saying unto him, Saul, Saul, why persecutest thou me? And he said, Lord, what wilt thou have*

108

me to do?" Look at Saul going from bad to good through God's timing. *And the Lord said, I am Jesus whom thou persecutest: it is hard for thee to kick against the pricks. And he trembling and astonished said, Lord, what wilt thou have me to do? And the Lord said unto him, Arise, and go into the city, and it shall be told thee what thou must do"* God told Ananias to go to straight street to meet Saul and lay hands on him, that Saul might receive his sight. Ananias was skeptical about carrying out the task. God told Ananias, *"For he is a chosen vessel unto me, to bear my name before the Gentiles, and kings, and the children of Israel"* (Acts 9:3-4, 6b, 5b, 6c, 15). There is something about the presence of God that humbles us, and it happens very quickly. Saul was riding on a horse with great authority, once he encountered God's presence, he ended up on the ground.

Zacchaeus was a tax collector of the city of Jericho that was greedy and crooked. He heard that Jesus was passing through the city, so he ran ahead of the crowd and climbed up in a sycamore tree to get a close up of Jesus because Zacchaeus was short in stature. After Jesus saw Zacchaeus in the tree, He told him to make haste and come down because He was going to abide at his home. Zacchaeus was very happy, but the crowd complained that Jesus had gone to be a guest of a sinner. When Jesus arrived at Zacchaeus home, he immediately said, *"The half of my goods, I give to the poor and if I defrauded anyone of anything, I restore it twofold."* Zacchaeus proved that his repentance and faith are genuine. Jesus announced that salvation had come to Zacchaeus's home. He went from Bad to Good, through God's timing.

Miriam and her brother gossiped about Moses marrying a Cushite. Moses was a very humble man, humbler than anyone else on the face of the earth. Miriam's story encourages us to continually trust in God. Miriam led the Israelite women in praise, worshipping God for His deliverance, after He parted the Red Sea. We are called to praise God and thank Him through the trials and the triumphs alike. Miriam was known for doing a bad thing, until God punished her with leprosy. However, she also did many good things, including saving a nation and protecting her baby brother Moses by placing him in a basket on the Nile River.

The Prodigal Son told his father he wanted his inheritance now and left home. He lost everything and went down. He was so poor, hungry, and desperate until he was willing to eat the slop from the pigs, even though he was Jewish. The Bible says, *"And when he came to himself, he said, How many hired servants of my father's have bread enough and to spare, and I perish with hunger! I will arise and go to my father, and will say unto him, Father, I have sinned against heaven, and before thee. And am no more worthy to be called thy son: make me as one of thy hired servants. And the son said unto him, Father, I have sinned against heaven, and in thy sight, and am no more worthy to be called thy son. For this my son was dead, and is alive again; he was lost, and is found. And they began to be merry" (Luke 15:17-19, 21,24).* A wasteful son became a grateful son.

The Woman at the Well would always go at noon time to get her water, although it was not an opportune time, because it was during the heat of the day when other women would not meet at that time to socialize. So, the woman at the well chose that time of day because of her reputation and promiscuous lifestyle, and she did not want to be taunted and sneered at by the other women as an outcast. One day she met Jesus at the well and Jesus told her to give him some water to drink. She was shocked because the Jews had no dealings with the Samaritans, because they worshipped idol gods. The Bible says, *"Jesus answered and said unto her, If thou knewest the gift of God, and who it is that saith to thee, Give me to drink; thou wouldest have asked of him, and he would have given thee living water" (John 4:10).* Jesus told the Samaritan woman if you drink of the water that you are getting you will thirst again, but If you drink of the water that He has to give, He told her she will never thirst again, because the water He has to give her, would be a well of water springing up into the everlasting life. Jesus told her to go and get her husband and she responded to Him that she did not have one. He told her she had five husbands and the one she is with now is not her husband. The woman left her water pot and went into the city and said, *"Come see a man, which told me all things that ever I did: is not this the Christ" (John 4:29).* In the end, this woman used her gift and calling to introduce other women to Jesus. She became a disciple and evangelist instantly. Society saw her as an outcast, but Jesus saw her need for salvation and deliverance. The Living Christ looked beyond her faults and saw her needs.

The Philippine Jailer had received charge over Paul and Silas in jail. He thrust them into the inner prison and locked their feet in the stocks. At midnight, Paul and Silas prayed and sang praises unto God. God sent an earthquake to shake the prison. All the doors were opened, and everyone's bands were loosed. The Philippine Jailer woke up and saw what was happening, drew out his sword to himself because he knew he was going to be in trouble for letting the prisoner flee. Paul cried with a loud voice, *"Do thyself no harm, for we are all* here" *(Acts: 16:28)*. The jailer fell down before Paul and Silas, and asked what must he do to be saved. He and all his household believed and were saved. They all broke bread together.

Ruth left her paganistic country to follow her mother-in-law who had lost her husband and two sons, which one of the sons was married to Ruth. Naomi, her mother-in-law, went back to Bethlehem, the house of Bread. Naomi begged Ruth to stay in Moab because she was too old to have anymore children. Ruth had compassion for Naomi, knowing she was an older widow woman and did not have anyone to depend on. Ruth insisted that she would follow Naomi back to her country and these are the words she told Naomi, *"Intreat me not to leave thee, or to return from following after thee: for whither thou goest, I will go; and where thou lodgest, I will lodge: thy people shall be my people, and thy God my God. Where thou diest, will I die, and there will I be buried: the Lord do so to me, and more also, if ought but death part thee and me" (Ruth 1:16-17)*. Ruth immediately joined up with Naomi, her country, and her lifestyle, but above all, her religion. Because Ruth, out of love for her widowed mother-in-law, was willing to give up everything—her family, her culture, and her pagan religion— to support her during times of weakness and vulnerability, God blessed Ruth by leading her to be chosen by the richest man in the country to become his wife. Through this union, Ruth was able to enjoy the best of life with Naomi, now through her husband. This was the best life that these two ladies could ever dream of. It pays to forget about yourself and think of others. Ruth went from a Moabitess to an Israelite. She was blessed in every aspect of her life.

Apollos was a Jew, born in Alexandria. He was an elegant man and mighty in the scriptures, who went to Ephesus, where he is described as being fervent in spirit. Apollus was an influential teacher and leader who advanced the gospel of Jesus in the early Christian church. He had been instructed in the way of the Lord and with great enthusiasm. Apollos spoke and taught accurately about the facts about Jesus, although he knew only the baptism of John. He did not have any knowledge of the Holy Spirit. He began to speak boldly in the synagogue. When Aquilla and Priscilla heard him, they took him aside and explained to him the way of God accurately or more perfectly. They did it with discretion and invited him to their home, rather than trying to show him publicly. Apollos humbled himself and listened. We can always increase in our learning, no matter how big our audience is or our circle, there is always room for improvement. I love this scripture: *"I have planted, Apollos watered; but God gave the increase. So then neither is he that planteth any thing, neither he that watereth; but God that giveth the increase. Now he that planteth and he that watereth are one: and every man shall receive his own reward according to his own labour"* (1 Corinthians 3:6-8).

CHAPTER TWELVE
Repentance...Forgiveness...Obedience

Philemon was a very wealthy man from Colossae, who was a follower of Jesus. He had a slave named Onesimus, who ran away from him after he had done Philemon wrong. When Onesimus met Paul, he repented of his sin and immediately became a follower of Jesus as well. Paul writes a letter to Philemon requesting that he forgives Onesimus and welcome him as a brother in Christ and not as a slave. We learned from Philemon's story the importance of forgiveness. It also teaches us that we should forgive those who have sinned against us, even when they have done us wrong. Paul paid Philemon back from Onesimus's wrongness.

Abraham is considered the father of the Jewish nation. He obeyed God and went to the land of Canaan. Abraham was an idolater who God called to leave his homeland, family, and friends. Abraham deviated a little and carried his nephew with him. His nephew carried his loved ones, livestock, and servants. Abraham had to pay for not obeying God wholeheartedly. He realized his mistake, although it caused him much grief, disappointments, and burdens. God had mercy on him and saw him through. No sin goes unpunished. Abraham was punished through his own mistakes, but he still carried out the will of God. Abraham teaches us the importance of obedience. We cannot win against God's plan or timing. When we follow God, He will bless us.

Peter denied Jesus three times before the rooster crowed, but he repented and was forgiven. Jesus had already told him that he would deny Him three times. Peter loved Jesus, but he feared for his life when he saw that they were going to take Jesus's life. He followed Jesus afar off. He said he did not know Jesus and he even cussed to prove that he had no connection to Him. Later, Peter went on to become one of the most influential apostles. *Jesus asked Peter, "Who do you say I am?" Peter replied, "You are the Christ, the Son of the living God." Jesus told Peter, "For flesh and blood and has not revealed this to you, but my father who is in heaven did." Jesus said, "And I say also unto thee, That thou art Peter, and upon this rock I will build my church; and the gates of hell shall not prevail against it. And I will give unto thee the keys of the kingdom of heaven: and whatsoever thou shalt bind on earth shall be bound in heaven: and whatsoever thou shalt loose on earth shall be loosed in heaven" (Matthew 16:18-19).* Peter preached on the day of Pentecost and 3000 people were saved. We can learn from Peter and a loving God that He is always willing to forgive us and use us for His purposes, even when we fail or deny Him.

Of the thieves on the cross, one of them mocked Jesus and said, "If thou be Christ, save thyself and us." The other thief rebuked the outspoken thief and said, "Do thou fear God, seeing thou art in the same condemnation? He told the other thief, "We are receiving the due reward of our deeds that we have done but this man hath done nothing amiss." He told Jesus, "Lord, remember me when thou comest into thy

Kingdom." Jesus told the repentant thief, "Verily I say unto thee, today shalt thou be with me in paradise." That thief knew to humble himself and repent to receive forgiveness. The other thief let pride overrule his thoughts and he was lost.

Lydia was known as a "dealer in purple cloth." She was a successful businesswoman and very, very hospitable. After Lydia converted over to Christianity, she opened her home to Paul and his companions, the workers of the Lord. Lydia and her family listened to the gospel, and it touched her heart, and because of that, she and her family got baptized. Lydia was among the women who were at the riverside who heard the gospel which Paul preached. She was moved by it and abided there because God opened her spirit to receive the gospel. She ushered her entire family to follow her to Christ. She told Paul to come into her house and abide there. She was known as the first convert to the Christian faith in the Roman city of Phillipi. She was known as a godly businesswoman, playing a significant role as an early and vital member of the church. She gave direction, leadership, and took charge in a situation with the most powerful leader in the New Testament Church, Paul. Lydia became the first female pastor of perhaps the very first household church in Europe. Lydia was obedient to God's Word. She repented of her sin. She exemplified hospitality. God can use anyone to further His kingdom, no matter their occupation.

These passages are important for us because it demonstrates how through the work of Jesus, salvation is extended not only to the Jews, but to everyone that believeth and receiveth. Jesus, who is our big brother and Great High Priest, makes intercession for us, establishing a new covenant relationship between God and man. Through Jesus's sacrifice, our sins are atoned for, and we are given new life, living in the fullness of His grace. When you look at the story of the woman at the well, it demonstrates that Jesus comes to the least of these. He cares for the outcasts of society. The woman at the well also known as the Samaritan woman, was considered inferior because of her sex, ethnicity, and relationship history, but none of that mattered to Jesus because he saw her need for salvation. We can honestly say that God can save us no matter our circumstances, and that we do not need to overcome our sins with our own power before coming to Him. As we spread the Gospel through our daily walk, we must remember to share it openly to all, even those whom society deems the lowest and unworthy to consider.

We can also conclude that Jesus satisfies not only our physical needs but our spiritual needs as well. If we follow Jesus, we can rest in the promise that the troubles of this world are temporary. God will give us the power to endure them through the power of the Holy Spirit and have eternal hope in Christ.

CHAPTER THIRTEEN

But When the Fullness of Time Had Come...God's Appointed Time and the Set Time.

God sent ten plagues to Egypt and its Pharaoh, while the Israelites were there. God is an awesome God. The plagues only tormented and destroyed the Egyptians, while the Israelites remained unaffected. The plagues were ten disasters sent upon Egypt by God to convince Pharaoh to free the Israelites from bondage and oppression they had endured in Egypt for four hundred years. God sent Moses to deliver the children of Israel from bondage in Egypt. God promised to show His wonders as confirmation of Moses' authority. God wanted the confirmation to serve at least two purposes, to show the Israelites that the God of their fathers was alive and worthy of their worship and to show the Egyptians that their gods were nothing. The Israelites were discouraged and had lost their faith in the God of their fathers, because they were slaves for four hundred years for the Egyptians. They believed God existed and worshipped Him, but they had doubts that He could, or would deliver them out of Egypt.

According to Exodus 5:2, when Moses approached Pharoah, demanding that he let the people go, Pharaoh responded by saying, *"Who is the Lord, that I should obey his voice to let Israel go? I know not the Lord, neither will I let Israel go."* **This was the fullness of time, the set time, the appointed time.** God proved himself strong on the Israelites' behalf. He used ten plagues.

The first plague was turning the Nile River to blood. The river which formed the basis of daily life, and the national economy was devasted, as missions of fish died in the river and the water was unusable. God let it be known to Pharoah, *"By this you will know that I am the Lord" (Exodus 7:17).* **This was the fullness of time, the set time, the appointed time.** The second plague brought frogs from Nile River. They invaded every part of the homes of the Egyptians only. When the frogs died, their stinky bodies were heaped up in offensive piles all through the land as told in Exodus 8:13-14. The third plague was gnats. This plague was unique, it was not like the first two plagues. The magicians were unable to duplicate this plague and told Pharoah, *"This is the finger of God" (Exodus 8:19).* The fourth plague was flies. God clearly distinguished between the Israelites and the Egyptians. There were no flies swarming around nor did they bother the Israelites among their living quarters as written in Exodus 21-24. The fifth plague was the death of livestock. Yet, God still protected His people from the plague, while the Egyptians' cattle died. The Egyptians had a big loss in their economy because their livestock was destroyed. God proved himself strong toward the Israelites by protecting and providing for those who obeyed Him. Pharaoh could not fathom what he was witnessing. Exodus 9:7 says that he sent investigators to find out if the Israelites were suffering along with the Egyptians. His heart was hardened even more against the Israelites. The sixth plague was boils. The Bible says that the magicians "could not stand before Moses, because of the boils." Pharaoh's religious leaders had no power against the God of Israel. Before God sent the last three plagues, Pharaoh was given a special message from God. It shows you God loves the unlovely. The upcoming plagues would be more severe than the others, and they were designed to convince Pharaoh to gather whatever cattle and crops remained from all the previous plagues and shelter them from the coming storm. Some of Pharaoh's servants took heed and some did not. It reminds you of when the ark was being built, they had so many warnings, they ignored them and made fun. (Exodus 9:20). The seventh plague was hail. This hail was unlike any that had been seen before. This plague was accompanied by a fire which ran along the ground, and everything left out in the open was devastated by the hail and fire. Again, the children of Israel were miraculously protected, and no hail damaged anything on their property. God said in His Word, wherever He sees blood, He will pass there over. Before God sent the next plague, He told Moses that the Israelites would be able to tell their children of the things they had seen God do in Egypt and how it showed them God's power. All that the Israelites had witnessed helped to increase their faith, and they learned more and more about God in all His glory and power. The eighth plague, God sent locusts again. The crops that had come up later, which had survived the hail, was wheat and rye. They were devoured by the swarms of locusts. Egypt did not have any harvest that year. The ninth plague was darkness. For three days the land of Egypt was smothered with an unearthly darkness, but the homes of the Israelites had light all three days. The tenth and last plague, the death of the first-born males, was a judgement. In this plague, God taught the Israelites a deep spiritual lesson that would point them to Christ. The tenth plague the children of Israel had to have an act of faith. God commanded each Israelite family to take an unblemished male lamb and kill it. God gave them directions that the blood of the lamb was to be roasted and eaten that night. The Israelites were told, anyone that did not follow God's instructions would suffer in the last plague. God described how He would send the destroyer through the Land of Egypt, with orders to slay the first-born male in every household, whether they were human or animal. The only protection that the Israelites would have would be the blood of the lamb on their door. When the destroyer saw the blood, he would pass over that house and leave it untouched. (Exodus 12:23) This is how the Passover came about. Passover is a memorial of that night in ancient Egypt when God delivered His people from bondage. 1 Corinthians 5:7 teaches that Jesus became our Passover when He died to deliver us from the bondage of sin. While the Israelites found God's protection in their homes, every other home in the Land of Egypt experienced God's wrath as their loved ones died. This was the plague that caused Pharoah to finally release the Israelites.

When the Israelites left Egypt, they had a clear picture of God's power, protection, and plan for them. Some of the Israelites were willing to believe they had convincing evidence that they served the true and living God. However, some still failed to believe, which led to other trials and lessons by God.

Even after the tenth plague, Pharaoh hardened his heart again and sent his chariots after the Israelites. God opened a way through the "Red Sea" for the Israelites. The Egyptians pursued them, and Pharaoh's armies—all of them drowned. The power of Egypt was crushed, and the fear of God spread through the surrounding nations (Exodus 14:21-31). This was the very purpose that God had declared at the beginning, to show the Israelites that the God of their fathers was alive and worthy of their worship and to show the Egyptians that their gods were useless and unworthy. Even as believers today, we can reflect on those events to confirm our faith in and our fear of, this true and living God, the Judge of all the earth. **But when the fullness of time had come, the set time, and the appointed time, God delivered the children of Israel out of slavery and bondage and showed them signs of wonders. God had an appointed time, a set time, for them to cross the Red Sea without any harm. They had to experience the ten plagues, but they had no harm done to them like the Egyptians suffered. God set the time and the limits on our tests until the fullness of time for us to receive deliverance and the victory.**

Nebuchadnezzar is known as the greatest king of Babylon. He made Babylon a splendid city. He destroyed the temple of Jerusalem and initiated the Babylonian captivity of the Jewish population. Nebuchadnezzar got caught up in pride while in the comfort of his palace. He began to boast and brag, "Look how great Babylon is. I built it as my capital city to display my power and my might, my glory, and my majesty." Before the words were out of his mouth, a voice from heaven said, "King Nebuchadnezzar, listen to what I say! Your royal power is now taken away from you. You will be driven away from human society, live with the wild animals and eat grass like an ox for seven years. Then you will acknowledge that the Supreme God has the power over everything and ruleth in the kingdom of men, and giveth it to whosoever He will. The same hour the prophecy was fulfilled upon Nebuchadnezzar. He was driven from men and did eat grass as oxen, and his body was wet with the dew of heaven till his hairs were grown like eagles' feathers and his nails like bird's claws. Who would have ever thought that God would have brought king Nebuchadnezzar down like that? **But when the fullness of time had come—the appointed time and the set time.** Nebuchadnezzar had a change of heart. He said he lifted his eyes unto heaven and his understanding returned unto him and he blessed the Most High and he praised and honored Him that liveth forever, whose dominion and his generation is everlasting from generation to generation. He declared that all the inhabitants of the earth are reputed as nothing, and that God does according to His will in the army of Heaven. No one can question God, "What doest thou?" At the same, Nebuchadnezzar reasoning returned to him, for the glory of his kingdom. God returned unto him his honor and brought him back in his kingdom and excellent majesty was added unto him. He was reestablished as king in his kingdom and became greater than ever. That is why Nebuchadnezzar sang, "I Nebuchadnezzar, sing and praise the King of Heaven." God said the high places He will bring down. He took Nebuchadnezzar all the way down, literally to the ground, until he humbled himself. God brought him back up even higher. That was his appointed time and the set time for him.

Job, a servant of God, has been fortunate with many blessings. Job had the ideal family, good health, and even abundant riches. He was very grateful and had a strong relationship with God. He did not take God's gifts for granted; he continued to love and thank God. God testified about Job. That will always cause others to pick on you or challenge you.

Satan asked God if he could tempt Job to see if he would remain faithful. God gave Satan permission, and Job began to experience many losses. Things that were dear to him were lost. He lost his animals, his property, his children, and then he endured constant pain in his body, being covered with sores and boils. The only person who survived was his wife, and Satan spoke through her, telling him to curse God and die. If that was not enough, his closest friends accused him of hidden sin, saying it was the reason for all these calamities. They sat with him for seven days without saying a word because he looked so terrible. After the seven days of silence, Eliphaz, Bildad, and Zophar openly accused him, saying God never allows the just to suffer. *"Yea, and all that will live godly in Christ Jesus shall suffer persecution"* (2 Timothy 3:12). Job told his miserable comforters he had not sinned. One of Job's famous lines is, *"I know that my Redeemer liveth"* (Job 19:25). **But when the fullness of time had come—the appointed time and the set time.** God eventually showed up in a great storm and did not accuse Job of anything. Instead, God condemned Job's three friends for speaking falsely and slandering His name. Job had been closer to God than his three friends. God told Job to pray for his sinning friends, and He rewarded Job with much more happiness than he had before. *"So the Lord blessed the latter end of Job more than his beginning, for he had fourteen thousand sheep and six thousand camels, and a thousand yoke of oxen, and a thousand she-asses. Job also had seven sons and three daughters. God gave Job the prettiest land. Job lived one hundred and forty years, and saw his sons, even four generations. So Job died, being old and full of days"* (Job 42:12-13, 15).

The story of a widow's olive oil is told in 2 Kings Chapter 4. This woman came to Elisha, the prophet who was at her wit's end. She was in desperation and her back was against the wall. She was very fearful because a creditor had threatened to take her two sons as slaves unless she paid the debt she owed. The prophet, Elijah, asked her, "What do you have in your house." She said, "Nothing but a small jar of olive oil." He told her to go around to all her neighbors and ask for their empty jars and ask for a lot. Then he told her to go inside and shut the door and pour the oil she had into each jar and put it over to the side. He told her after she had filled every jar to sell the olive oil and pay her debts and there would be enough money left over for her and her sons.

This woman had to have had faith and trust to believe the man of God. **But when the fullness of time had come— the appointed time and the set time.** Even in the midst of her own problems, she was a solution. God gave her supernatural abundance, resources, and provisions because she obeyed His Word. This widow was in an indebted state, but God made her an entrepreneur. She used what she had, despite how weak and afraid she felt, and the Lord turned her biggest misery into her greatest ministry. This is encouraging to us that He will do the same for us. We can learn a lot from this widow woman. She sought God's wisdom to gain a new perspective and used what she had, which was not much, to get what she needed. She only had one small jar of olive oil, but Elijah, the prophet, told her to pour it out. We do not need to hold on to something because we cannot see where the next supply will come from. God's mathematics is different from ours and He will multiply whatever our seed might be if we trust Him. She became a big distribution center for the

Kingdom of God because He was in it. She was able to seek resources from her neighbors and friends, and they invested in her new venture. Never be afraid to ask, the Bible says ask and it shall be given. She was able to sell her olive oil very quickly because it was something everyone needed at that time. God said, *"My grace is sufficient for thee: for my strength is made perfect in weakness. Most gladly therefore will I rather glory in my infirmities, that the power of Christ may rest upon me. Therefore I take pleasure in infirmities, in reproaches, in necessities, in persecutions, in distresses for Christ's sake: for when I am weak, then am I strong"* *(2 Corinthians 12:9-10).*

The woman with the issue of blood had suffered bleeding for twelve long years. She allowed many things from many physicians and had spent all that she had. The Bible says that nothing improved but rather grew worse. I would say that the physicians might have taken advantage of her. They knew she was a widow woman, and she was anxious to be healed. Imagine twelve years of going to the physician and seeing no results, yet money was leaving you and your bank account. The scripture says her condition got worse. This woman was discouraged and embarrassed by the Jewish culture. Any woman that stays on her menstrual cycle pass seven days is considered "unclean." No man would ever want to marry her. This woman was an outcast, but she still fought on. She did not give up or give in. She kept the faith that one day she would be healed, despite regretting the loss of twelve years' worth of hard-earned money. This woman took a big chance of being called down, called out, and isolated. When you keep your mind on Jesus, He will keep you in perfect peace, that is what she did, because all odds were against her.

One day this woman came up behind Jesus and touched the hem of His garment. **But when the fullness of time had come—the appointed time and the set time.** *"...Immediately the woman with the issue of blood for twelve long years, her hemorrhage stopped! Jesus wanted to know who touched Him. Peter being outspoken said, "Master, in a crowd like this, anyone could have pressed in on you." Jesus told Peter that it was a different touch, for He noticed the power had gone out from Him. When the woman heard that, she could not hold back and remain silent. She came trembling and fell at Jesus's feet, and said she touched Him and immediately her bleeding had stop. Jesus told the woman, "Your faith has made you well, go in peace"* (Luke 8:43-48).

The Shunamite woman from the village of Shumen, was a wealthy woman among her people, but she was barren or childless. Elisha was a prophet who often passed her home on his travels. The Shunamite woman knew he was a true prophet and holy man of God, by him staying in the guest room. This woman got permission from her husband, to set up a little chamber for him, with a bed table, stool, and a candlestick. Whenever he came to town, he would stay with them in this chamber.

Elisha asked his servant, Gehazi, how he would help the woman in return, for her sharing hospitality. I always tell people the more you give, the more you receive in return. There is a song that says, "If when you give, give the best of your service." God will do the rest. Elisha's servant told him that she had no son, and her husband was elderly. Elisha immediately called the woman and prophesied to her that she would have a son by that time next year. The prophecy came to pass like

Elisha prophesied, but it was several years later. The child came down with some kind of sickness and he died that same day in his mother's lap. She took her son and laid him in Elisha's bed and shut the door. She went and found Elisha and asked him to come back with her to see her son. **But when the fullness of time had come—the appointed time and the set time.** Elisha came into the house, where his chamber was and saw the dead son lying on his bed. He went in and shut the door. I noticed in the book of 2 Kings, it always talked about, "shut the door." Whenever God is giving us a visit, a prophecy, a Word, or an individual command, you are not to let everyone in on what is happening or about to take place until after the manifestation. Many people are fearful, doubtful, and discouraged, and will try to hinder the works of the Lord, some knowingly and some beknownest. Elisha went and prayed to the Lord, laid himself on the child, putting his mouth on his mouth, his eyes on his eyes, and his hands on his hands. As Elisha stretched himself upon him, the child became warm, and Elisha got up and walked away. He came back and stretched himself again on her son again. The child sneezed seven times and opened his eyes.

Elisha gave the woman another prophecy, telling her to depart with her household because a seven-year famine was coming. She obeyed the man of God and left with her family for seven years and then returned. She realized after coming back that she had lost her land due to the desertion of her property. Again, she used her faith and went to the king. The Bible says the heart of the king is in the Lord's hands and he channels it accordingly to His will. She went to the king in desperation about her losses. Elisha's servant told the king who the woman was, and how her son was restored to the life through Elisha. **But when the fullness of time had come—the appointed time and the set time.** The king appointed unto her a certain officer, to restore all that was hers and all the fruits of the field from the day that she left the land, even until then. Look at God how He blessed the Shunamite woman because she shared generously and offered hospitality to the man of God. She supported the work of God by acknowledging Elisha as a man of God, even though she was suffering from being childless, she still served the prophet.

Gideon was a very young lad. God chose a weak, fearful man. Gideon is characterized by fear and inadequacy. He had little or no confidence. God went to him as he was beating out wheat in a wine press. He is hiding because he is afraid. God called Gideon out of weakness. His character became bold and passionate, he was a leader with insight. He had the wisdom to see the issues and vision to see what lies ahead. God gave Gideon the insight into the weak hearts of the Midianites.

The Lord was angry with the Israelites for falling into sin and worshipping false gods and idols. Because of their disobedience, God left them in the hands of the destructive Midianites for seven years. Finally, the Israelites were helpless, and they cried out to God for help. God sent help through a young man named Gideon. The angel told Gideon he would deliver the Israelites from the Midianites and Gideon said, "I am just a young small boy." Gideon used a fleece test, to really see that God would be with him, and many men joined Gideon's army. God immediately told Gideon 22,000 army to be cut down, so the Israelites would not bring it was them that win the victory. They were cut down to 10,000, the Lord said, it was still too many. Gideon took the remaining down to the river and He told Gideon only to keep the people who drank like a dog. He had only 300 in his army to fight against the Midianites. You know that back in the Bible days that was not an army. **But when the fullness of time had come—the appointed time and the set time.** Gideon told his army to split into three groups. He gave each one trumpets and jars with torches in them. They marched to the Midianites camp, following Gideon's orders. They stood together shouting repeatedly, "A sword for the Lord and for Gideon." All the Midianites fled in terror. Gideon sent messengers to other Israelites about the Midianites, so the other Israelites captured the Midianites and killed their leaders. If God be for you, who can be against you! It will always stand that God and one are the majority.

CHAPTER FOURTEEN
But When the Fullness of Time Had Come for Me... the Appointed Time and the Set Time

I had planned to return for the first semester of school in August 2013 and retire at the end of December. The Board of Education told me that I did not have to wait to have all my years in, I could retire in the first week in September. That meant that I did not have to go back after Labor Day. My principal asked me if I would stay a little while longer at Whiteville High School and I wanted to stay until the end of the year, which would have been the big exodus for Christmas break. Nevertheless, whether he asked me or not, I had said I was going to finish the semester out. I did not want to leave my students wondering who their new teacher would be. When students have a lot of substitute teachers, they have the proclivity to get sidetracked, cut class, and then at the end, they want to blame the substitute teachers. God had always blessed me to have my students under control, so I was never one of those teachers that could not wait until 2:15 or the next holiday, break or teacher's seminar. I loved my students, and I looked forward to seeing them every day as if they were mine, unlike some of today's parents that do not want to see their children, hate the snow days, spring break, holiday break, and dread the summer months. That is a reflection on the parents, not doing their job in raising them properly, nor carrying them to church. So, when December 20, 2013, at 10:20 a.m., they announced my final hour had come. **But when the fullness of time had come for me—the appointed time and the set time.** They told me at the board, to go home and call in a substitute teacher for the first few days in January, and they would pay me for all of the holidays. I said, "Yes, Ma'am." Look at God. When God has a blessing with your name on it, it is yours, even if you are not cognizant of it. I did not think of that. I never would have thought of that, "But God!" The Board of Education officially made my retirement date January 2014. I was 57 years old and was clothed in my right mind. I walked in my career at 22 years old at Western High School and 35 years later I had become 57 when I walked out of Whiteville High.

But when the fullness of time had come—the appointed time and the set time. During my 35 years of teaching math, I just thought God put me in that field of study, because a math teacher is always needed at every level. Nevertheless, I taught math in twenty schools. It was very easy for me. It was like a piece of cake. I always had favor with all my principals, except one. Despite this, most of all, he held high regard and great respect toward me. *However, face to face, he showed me he did not care for me. "Woe to you when all men speak well of you" (Luke 6:26a).* When I told my math supervisor that, he was startled and told me the principal gave me great compliments and said if anyone from the board should visit him, he would always take them to my room. His one-on-one actions were far from what he expressed to me. At this age, I know that "respect" means more than "like."

When I first started teaching in the Kirby County School System, God placed me in schools where I had to stay on my toes. I had to establish many classroom rules at the beginning of the year, with some added along the way. Above all, I had to keep my prayer wheel turning to deal with unforeseen problems, expectancies, pop tests, and to keep my sanity, teaching 180 students a day, a hard-core subject, such as math. It seems as if God put me in all the schools that were surrounded by low-income housing projects. I loved my students so much and learned a lot from them, being in the "hood." For the most part, they had good hearts, but they had to fend for themselves. They kept a defense up, so they would not come across as being weak or a square. They would always bring the problems in the neighborhood to school, and parents would back them in their naughtiness. I was not just teaching regular students apt to learn. Many of my students arrived at school burdened by bitterness, lack of love, disappointments, and challenges such as being latchkey children. Sometimes they faced situations like no electricity or food at home, relying primarily on meals provided at school, which, while healthy, were not always their preferred choices. However, these meals were often better than nothing, especially when waiting for the next batch of food stamps, if their families did not sell too many of them. God allowed me to take a break every three years by leaving on my own will. At about seven of the schools I taught in, God gave me the mindset to return, and I was welcomed back by the principals with open arms. God was just giving me a break to a new neighborhood, a new way to go to work, new colleagues, parents, students, and communities, but the drain did not change. It shows you that God cares about every aspect and area of our lives if we have a daily relationship with Him and are on speaking bases with Him. I thank God I learned that an early age. God definitely showed results when I needed him most. *"O taste and see that the Lord is good" (Psalms 34:8 NIV).*

I worked in those questionable schools for approximately 10 years, but then God gave me a break and sent me to one of the top schools in a certain area of the city. I taught there for nine years. I had parent participation, school trip participation, and they were very involved and concerned about their child being college bound. After I left there, I had only sixteen years left in my career and God pulled the best out of me in teaching in various parts of the city. Some schools as I stated earlier, I went back and taught there for the second time. God was not through using me at those various schools. I went back gladly. That's when I realized that God was using me in ministry through teaching math. It became clear that I could leave a school whenever I felt led to do so, with ease. Different colleagues would ask me how I managed to do it, and my answer was always the same: it was God! **But when the fullness of time had come—the appointed time and the set time.**

When my 35 years were coming toward the big exodus of retirement, God put me in the number one school in the state of Tennessee and that is when I retired. I had three small classes consisting of 10-15 students. I was given two aides; one would teach, and the other one would grade papers and record their grades online. They gave my students pizza parties, and I just coasted my last years until retirement! One of the saints had come over to the school and told me to keep my door shut, so the other colleagues would not know what God had given me. Both of my aides had degrees in Math, and they were not novices or fly by night. You keep living for God and trust Him for everything, He will lighten the load and He will bring the high places down. **But when the fullness of time had come for me—the appointed time and the set time.** I had already retired and was only receiving one check from the Board of Education instead of two checks a month, when I was working. My bills were the same, but my income was less, considering one check a month, I was too young to draw social security, but I had purchased this big home, and it was extremely high maintenance. Nevertheless, Big God told me the home was mine. "Whose Report are you Going to Believe?" I needed some, and another income before I was able to receive full benefits from social security. I could not receive my husband's income, until I was sixty years old, had a death certificate, and marriage license. I went to get a death certificate as his wife, but they said his death certificate said that I was unknown. That is why it is so important to have a day-to-day relationship with God, because God has the final say. I did not fight what the death certificate had said, I knew I had the marriage license to shut down all doubts. I brought the marriage certificate to show proof with the original seal. It was an appointed time and a set time for me, for my husband to be called by God. It was that very year that he died, that I turned sixty years old, and I started to receive his big total social security because it went to his parent's house a day after he died. They did not cash or spend it. In case anything went wrong, they would not have to pay it back. God saw fit that the wife (me), would receive it. I knew nothing about it, neither knew the day of each month he received. Social Security sent me a letter with the full amount and his burial fee. I said, "My God, How Great Thou Art!" I have been receiving this check every month for the last eight years. Timing is everything with God. That was my fullness of time, my appointed time, and my set time to receive his income and that became my second check. While I was trying to figure out my income, God had already worked it out. **But when the fullness of time had come to me—the appointed time and the set time.** I had borrowed $52,000 from Joy Land Bank because I was a desperate sister, financially strapped and again at my wits end. I was at a place in my life that I had never experienced. It was definitely a real wilderness experience. It was unknown and uncomfortable, but that was my tailored-made test, sent from God. He carried me through every step of the way, He did not leave me out there to fend for myself. The more I fasted, He would come and see about me. The fasting and praying did not change the condition because I had to pass my test and go through it, or I would have to go through that test again. My praying and fasting conditioned me for the change. It did not change the condition, again it conditioned me for the change. I was able to endure hardness as a good soldier. Instead of me asking the Lord to get me out of the test, I got better results by asking the Lord, "What do you want me to get out of the test." All of our tests should come to make us better not bitter, draw us closer to God, our test should be our testimony.

I was in prayer on a Thursday night at home at approximately 7:00 p.m. when I received a call, and they told me they were calling from Joy Land Bank, and that if I would pay $7,000 in full by six months from then, they would disregard the $45,000 I owed. Well, I know banks do not call you at seven o'clock at night, telling you, we know you borrowed $52,000 but just pay back $7,000. I told them if it was not a hoax, send it to me in writing. A few days later, a letter did follow, and I called to make sure it was true. I scuffled to get $7,000 in six months, but God made it happen. God, Jehovah Jireh, El Roi, Thou God seeth me, literally gave me $15,000 dollars that I did not ever have to pay back. That was definitely a commanded blessing from God. Man did not give it to me, and man cannot take it away. What a Mighty God we serve! I just want to take time, seventeen years, and give him, "ADORATION." Lord, I adore you, I exalt you, I love you; you are my All and All. You are more than enough. You are my everything. You are my strength. You are my deliverer. You are my Father. You are my Hightower. You are the Multi-Breaster One. You are Elohim. You are more than enough. You are El Shaddai. I can go on and on about God. There are not enough words in the dictionary to describe our creator. **But when the fullness of time had come for me—the appointed time and the set time.** I had heard about Martha's Vineyard over the years, but I never dreamed of having the opportunity to go and have my golden friend traveling with me. Now I can truly say, God had a plan and a way that I would find this flyer for a nine-day trip to Martha's Vineyard, New York, Connecticut, New Jersey, Pennsylvania, Ohio, Massachusetts, Rhode Island, and Kentucky. I told my golden friend, and she was so excited about going. Normally, she does not like long trips, but God was in the plan. We paid our money, and I also invited my best friend. She came aboard and paid her money immediately. The three of us were so excited about going to Martha's Vineyard and touring the East Coast. We purchased new gear for the different events and enjoyed doing that before we left for the trip. We were so, so excited. The three of us were going places we had never been, neither was it on our bucket lists. While on the trip, we took lots of pictures, had a great time, met so many new people, and led prayers on the bus. We bonded and had the time of our lives because God knew there would be a big change in my life. **But when the fullness of time had come for my roommate—the appointed time and the set time.** God planned that too for us on purpose, the three of us. We probably will not get that opportunity and time again for the three of us. God knew when we got back from our trip that my roommate would be moving out four months later, coming into her very own blessings. God blessed her to live in gated community, all first floors, all new furniture, and a brand-new luxury SUV. Her timing was so smooth that you could tell that God was in it. We went and picked out furniture and her brand-new Cadillac SUV. God had really poured out on her in a mighty big way. Her sons and brother were right there to accommodate her and make her comfortable. They stayed the entire course, even though they had busy schedules and families. When God is in something, He sets the timing. It was marvelous in my eyes, and I was so happy. She had money to meet all of her needs. She had really calculated and saved up well. She is so, so happy. God has closed that chapter for her and gave her a whole new beginning after she had reached her seven-year completion. God had already instructed me to replace all the old carpet with new carpeting in my home. I agreed, and then He directed me to renovate the entire kitchen—making any changes necessary. I did not know she would be leaving at that time, doing those tasks was a great distraction for me so I would not feel the brunt of being left behind. We always said we would live together. God said differently. That was not His appointed time or set time for me, because I am still here. Her income was a great blessing to me and this household. She really appreciated her stay with me, because she did things that were not asked of her, like clockwork. God told me that I would be a blessing and receive a blessing. We both benefited from each other in a magnificent way. I really miss her and all the support she added to my home to maintain its status. She had taken me out to dinner two months before she left. At the restaurant, she had given her monthly allowance to me in cash. She left and took care of her business. I left and went to the post office to mail four letters. In the middle of those letters I had put the money she'd given me in between because she gave it to me in a white bank envelope. When I got to the mailbox at the post office, I dropped my letters in the mail slot along with the bank envelope with all of the cash inside. I did not realize what had happened until the next day. By that time, the local post office had carried all the mail bags to the main post office downtown. I went to both post offices and called the lost and found. Of course, no one had turned it in. You know how people think when they do not practice integrity, they feel like that is their blessing! All of the cash was in hundred-dollar bills. I'm sure they were excited and could not believe their eyes and took a chance and put it in their pockets, not caring that they were under surveillance even though they knew two people got fired from taking from the mail. I told my pastor about it, and he said that maybe God wants me to see how it feels if my roommate would get her own place. Not knowing that God was speaking through him. She did not know and neither did I, that her departure would be in two months, because the place where she is currently staying, told her that she would have to wait until something became available. **But God had a set time and an appointed time for her**, and that time was in two months. God was in it, and He helped her every step of the way. She had taken care of three widow women with all of her heart. God rewarded her for her works and did not forget about her labor of love. All that she had put in the church, sowing seeds, tithes, and offerings, He gave it back to her. God does not need our money. He is the one that gave man the knowledge to make it. God wants to see if we are going to obey Him. Paying tithes, offerings, and sowing seeds are an act of obedience to His command. God gave her both her cake and ice cream at the same time. She is Shining So!

I lost my father a few years earlier, and then I lost my sister, mom, and husband all within eight days. I knew they were not coming back. I was working everyday with high school students, so I had to deal with the challenges at hand, so I did not have time to grieve, I had to focus on my career and help my seniors graduate on time. I did not mourn and grieve like the world. The Bible says that you should only grieve for thirty days. *"And the children of Israel wept for Moses in the plains of Moab thirty days, so the days of weeping and mourning for Moses were ended" (Deuteronomy 34:8)*. Everybody grieves differently, but God said He will wipe all your tears away. *"Weeping may endure for a night, but joy comes in the morning" (Psalms 30:5)*. When my roommate left, I was in a different place in life than I was when my other loved ones left for good. I was a retiree, which means I had time to focus on everything that was at hand. I faced reality without any interruptions because I was at home everyday in quietness. The Bible says in quietness and confidence shall be your strength. Her leaving had an impact on me, and she was still living unlike the others. I had a few sad days, but God gave me strength to endure. We grew up together from the ages of six years old up to well into our sixties. We did a lot of things together. People thought we were sisters, and some thought we were even twins. She is happy and contented and I am happy and contented. God never makes a mistake. That chapter of our lives has ended. A good time was had by both, in spite, regardless of, and because of. She was and is a forever friend. God will put people in your life; some for a reason, some forever, and some for a season. I wish her all the best in the world and God's choice blessings from me and all my siblings. *We bid her God speed for life.* **But when the fullness of time had come—the appointed time and the set time!**

As I mentioned earlier, God had put in my spirit to redo some things in my home, so I wanted my floor to be redone and my fireplace. I did not know where to start looking and I did not have anything to compare prices with. I went to the store that had big commercials and with the little jingle songs. I thought I would start there first, not knowing that would be the only start I would use and need. I had a young man to assist me, and I told him to take me straight to the discounts. They had some flooring for $1.66 per square ft. I said, "This is it, and I love the color." He said it was discounted so low because it was a discontinued item. **The appointed time and set time was at hand.** I bought all I needed and was told they had marble tile for the fireplace to match the floor. It was almost four times the price of what I was paying for the flooring. I told him it was okay because I was receiving an unheard discount already. Then I needed someone whose price would be reasonable to remove the old and haul it away and install the new. They had about fifteen cards at the counter of businessmen who specialized in that type of work. I just picked up the first card I saw. We know the steps of a righteous man is ordered by God. That turned out to be an excellent choice.

He had a team of people to do the job in two days and then painted my mailbox for free. They took good care of my white furniture and baby grand piano that I was so concerned about. I would recommend those team of people to the "White House Officials" on Pennsylvania Drive in Washington, D.C. When you wait, work, and walk in God's timing, you are sure to have favor and success, because God is in it. **Amen.**

CHAPTER FIFTEEN
This Appointed Time Led Me to Great Finances

I n 2006, I was diagnosed with Pulmonary Hypertension. I was at the Holy Convocation in Memphis, Tennessee at the FedEx Forum. One of my best friends, also known as my golden friend from a sixty-two-year friendship, was with me. We decided to leave our seats and take a break. We ran up the stairs of the Forum, which were about thirteen to fifteen steps. When I got to the top of the last step, I collapsed. When I came to, several people were standing over me praying and pleading the blood of Jesus. I remember it as if it were yesterday. There was a gentleman with a very distinct northern accent, who said loud and clearly, "What is your name? What city are you in? Who is the President of the United States?" At this point they saw that I was coherent, and they stood me up. I told my golden friend, "Let's Go." A very tall, well-dressed gentleman, said very authoritatively, "Ma'am, we are sending you to the hospital." I softly told him that I did not want to go the hospital and that I was not going. He told me these words, "Oh yes, you are going, the ambulance is on its way. It is my job to send you, if not, I will lose my job." I knew then, the case was closed, and I had no further words. The paramedics were coming down the hall

144

swiftly with the stretcher. They put me on the stretcher and rushed me to the ambulance and carried me to Baptist East Hospital. My golden friend could not go with us, plus I did not need anyone at this point. She took the keys to the car and went home. I told her not to alarm anyone, and she did not. I needed to know what happened and what was going on with me. Sometimes if you call and tell people, they will beat the ambulance to the hospital and bombard the waiting room. The next day, my mom came and that was enough for me. My dad was already deceased at that time. They ran two or three tests and diagnosed me with Pulmonary Hypertension. The doctor explained to me what it was. I did not know anymore then, then before he told me. They finally put me on medication and told me to see my primary care physician right away.

Meanwhile, I am a researcher, regardless of what you tell me. I went home and got on my computer and looked up Pulmonary Hypertension. It is a type of high blood pressure that affects arteries in the lungs and in the heart. The symptoms are increased shortness of breath, fatigue, edema or swelling of the feet, legs, and eventually the abdomen and neck, dizziness and fainting spells, chest pain, heart palpitations, lips and fingers turning blue, and cough. Well, I thank God with my daily prayer life, reading His Word, fasting, and not forsaking my assembling at church each week, I did not have an encounter with the majority of the symptoms. I mostly had shortness of breath with exertion. I thank God for lightening my load along the way. The only understanding I had for a very long time was, most people have heart hypertension, which is considered as high blood pressure. So, I said they have diagnosed me with pulmonary hypertension which is high blood pressure in the lungs. I said, oh well, I used to have hypertension of the heart. They gave me a pill to take daily and that eradicated all of that. My blood pressure would always lie between 117 or less over 72 or less. Therefore, I was thinking pulmonary hypertension will be the same except instead of the heart, it's the lungs. That was 2006 and day by day would pass, month by month would pass, then all of a sudden, I would feel so tired. The Lord would bless, it really would not show up at school that much when I was teaching. I would really notice it during the school's fire drills, when we would have only a few minutes to clear the building. I would huff and puff all the way out the building and huff and puff all the way back inside to my classroom with my students all around me. I still did not think much of my diagnosis, because I knew I had climbed two flights of stairs going out of the building and coming in the building. The Lord had my mind turned that way so I would not really focus on the real situation.

As time went on, I noticed something was not right, because other teachers and students would climb the same flights with their books on their backs. I never noticed them huffing and puffing like me, not even the students that were larger than me in size. Again, I wrote it off as life. When I would leave school and visit my mom, I would feel so tired for no reason. Again, the side effects never rested on my mind. God said He would keep you in perfect peace, whose mind is stayed on Him. My prayer life and prayer wheel were turned up to the maximum. I made sure I got up an extra hour earlier to pray and read the Bible before I left for work. I saw the effects daily, and that is why I put forth an effort to get up early to have my spiritual devotion, talk to God in prayer, and let Him talk back to me in reading His Word.

By doing this every morning, I was able to handle unexpected events, pop quizzes, and irrational tasks. God blessed me to endure hardness as a good soldier, come what may.

Several years had passed and I would tell my primary doctor about my health issues, and he told me to see a pulmonologist. I googled that long hard word and that is why my understanding became clear. Reality had kicked all the way in. The pulmonologist ordered several tests on me and finally after she studied all my tests, she realized she would be seeing me for a while. She was curious how I chose her as my doctor. I told her I did not know who to pick. I just did the "Eeny Meeny Miny Moe," and we have been friends ever since. She is very knowledgeable, well read and very thorough in her field of pulmonary. She is very professional but outgoing as well. She is approachable too. I took several stress tests, treadmill tests, and sleep apnea tests, with her trying to get to the root of the matter. Finally, I was told that I was administered the wrong medication and that is what caused my diagnosis. I googled that as well. After googling that, a law firm appeared on screen. It said, "If you have any of these symptoms, call this number, 24 hours a day." I was reluctant to call. I thought it was a hoax, so I did not call. A few days later, I decided to look into it and see what it was all about. Folk, I tell you, it was nobody but God, setting me up to be blessed. I called the number which was the biggest law firm in the South. The attorney told me she would fly to my city and for me to pick the meeting place. She told me she would meet me at my job. I was so afraid. I did not know where this would lead and who I could discuss this with that I could trust. Everything was happening so fast. I told the attorney to meet me at my home. She had a gentleman to pick her up from the airport and bring her to my home. He stayed and waited the entire time, with the motor running for approximately an hour and a half. She was a very young attorney in her early thirties, but powerful with knowledge. She knew how to drill and probe me for information. At the end of our time together, she told me I had a case and was entitled to compensation. When she left and got back on the plane, I was speechless and in a daze. She told me not to talk to anyone and only communicate with her and her team. I still could not believe it, even though my best friend had prophesied that I would be a millionaire one day.

So, the law firm stayed in contact with me and kept me informed. They gave me their number to call for any reason or thought. They sent me a check for $200 each month to show me they had my case. I still did not tell anyone because I did not know what to say or how to say it. People will ask you so many questions out of curiosity and the unknown. I did everything they told me to do. The law firm kept in touch with me monthly and constantly gave me updates. They sent me a letter that they were going to have court in my home with the company they were suing. This was very mind boggling. I did not know what to expect. I also did not know how many people would be in my home. The attorney made sure I was privy to everything and everybody that would be in my home on that day. She told me everyone's role. I had two attorneys, two court reporters, and two clerks, of course. I was the one being represented. Everything was taped and videoed. My attorney gave me time to express myself. She told me to take my time and be very dramatic with my emotions. This was something for me to see and witness in the privacy of my own home. I continued to keep everything to myself as my attorney told me to.

My attorney told me that this was a big case, and it would probably take three years before I would be compensated. Three years seemed like an eternity to me, because I needed my mortgage paid as were speaking. My mortgage was $2,246.86 per month, coming from one salary, and that was from a teacher's salary, not a principal's salary, mind you. But God saw me through. He told me to keep my hands clean and He would sustain me. *"The Lord rewarded me according to my righteousness; according to the cleanness of my hands hath he recompensed me" (Psalm 18:20).* I made sure I kept my hands clean, because I did not want to lose my first brand new home. I did not have a boyfriend coming over, I was not drinking, nor did I let my home be a place where anything goes. I kept myself busy in His Word, praying, fasting, and going to church every week. As the saying goes, my money was funny, and my change was strange. I made sure I paid my tithes on time. I did not give God a tip, I gave Him His whole 10%, along with my offering. I knew it would be very foolish to rob God, who I was depending on to meet all my needs with His riches and glory. I gave no place to satan in lying, cheating, stealing, nor gossiping. I did not want my blessings to be held up, nor aborted. I kept a repenting heart and prayed daily talking to God. When I would read His Word, He would be talking to me. It is very essential and vital to have daily devotion with God, to maintain peace and joy. *"... in Thy presence is fullness of joy; at Thy right hand there are pleasures for evermore" (Psalm 16:11).*

Time traveled on and I kept on working every day. I noticed my health was not perfect, but I was able to care for myself, do for myself, teach every day, and travel every year. My health never got me down, but the symptoms were prevalent. I kept all my doctor's appointments and visits. My biggest symptom was shortness of breath with exertion and feeling tired. God gave me strength to endure hardness as a good soldier. I never had to use that as an excuse for not going to work or church. I was faithful to God and He was faithful to me. As I stated earlier, I did everything I wanted to do, and traveled extensively. I did go to the hospital twice when I moved into my home, because I kept going up and down stairs as if I were sixteen. That was not good for my lungs. I found out later that I overly exerted myself. Oftentimes, our minds are stronger than our bodies. When I would go to the hospital, I would drive myself, check myself in, and would stay a few days, while they run tests. They told me to slow down and stay active with my primary care and pulmonologist doctors and I did.

Meanwhile, my attorney was still calling and giving me updates and I would keep them informed about my health. They began to keep in contact with my doctors and involved them too. They were willing to be involved because they were being compensated as well. They would keep tests records and documents and kept my attorneys informed of every little thing. I really did not have time to focus on my health; my eyes and my mind saw nothing but dollar signs. How much it would be, I did not know, but my attorney said everything would be settled in three years. It was just like she said, actually two and a half years. It seemed as if my mortgage and car notes were coming every two weeks instead of once a month. God had one of my friends to see me through. She paid several mortgages and car notes, with no strings attached. She did not know I had a settlement coming to me. That is why it is so important to help people and give the best of your service. You will get it back, a lot of times, it does not come through the person you helped. In this case, this person was blessed by me and my entire family. Sometimes people forget what you have done and will be a bigger blessing to someone who thought little of them.

God said go in his vineyard and work, and whatever is right, he will pay. *"For God is not unrighteous to forget your work and labour of love, which ye have ministered to the saints, and do minister" (Hebrew 6:10)*. God remembers when others forget. *"The Lord shall count, when he writeth up the people" (Psalm 87:6a)*. That same lady bought me an airplane ticket for seven years straight, and paid for lodging, and most of my meals. I will never forget the kindness and love she showed toward me, taking me to New York for seven consecutive years. She asked if I would be the tour guide for the young ladies at her church, during Spring Break. She said these ladies needed a "getaway" and a change of scenery. Man, did I welcome that. I would carry my students to New York on Spring Break and that is how I learned New York like the back of my hand. God knows how to bless His people. I could not pay my mortgage or car notes, but I was traveling to the Big Apple, living large and I was literally in charge. I was living like I had oil wells pumping in my backyard. God knows how to cover you. No one knew my financial situation unless I told them. *"In quietness and in confidence shall be our strength" (Isaiah 30:15b)*.

Even though I had health issues, I did not go around with a sad countenance and a sad story. I kept on smiling and looking up, because God is Up. He was the one covering me. I placed my trust and faith in God. I kept wearing happy colors, which often caused people to stop and smile. Many times, I received positive feedback in the form of compliments. I never have been the kind of person when asked, "How are you?" And you tell the person about all your ailments and doctor's appointments and visits. When a person asks you "How are you," they are just being courteous. They do not want to be pressed down with your long drill of everything you are going through with your spouse, children, on the job, finances, and whatever is bringing you down. A lot of people are waiting to exhale. Just exhale with God. He is the only one that can fix your situation. Everyone has their own "row to how." The average person you meet, their teeth are on edge. Even now as I am writing this book, my teeth are on edge, but you would never know it. God said that we are the light of the world. The average person would rather be around a hundred-watt light bulb than a 20 watt, which is dull and dim, which can be very depressing. Nobody wants to be a dump truck where you dump all your trash on them and load them down with your burdens. When you are an ambassador for God, you are supposed to lift up and build up. Even when Jesus was on the cross, He said, "Father forgive them, for they know not what they are doing." He could have called legions of angels to deliver Him. He held His peace and endured His cross. Jesus knew talking about His misery or complaining was not going to be the solution. Let us learn from our perfect example, Jesus, not man. Man is fallible, but God is infallible.

As I am waiting on God's deliverance, my focus is on Him and not my issue. Mind you, my issue is ever before me, because I live in this body and my body is always with me. When you are walking with God, He is the one that is carrying you. When someone is carrying you, you do not feel the weight or the load of the burden. God has lightened my load and cooled the flames, just as He did for Daniel in the lion's den and for Shadrach, Meshach, and Abednego in the fiery furnace. These men were faithful to God, even when they were exiled to Babylon. King Nebuchadnezzar was stunned to see a fourth figure in the fire, recognizing Him as none other than the Son of God. The three Hebrew boys knew the risk involved and had no guarantee of deliverance, but their actions showed that they would rather face death than worship any false gods.

CHAPTER SIXTEEN
God's Preparation to My Appointed Time of Victories

I was at a weekly prayer meeting and a prophetess prayed for me and she said, "God is going to carry you across the bridge." Of course I was a bit startled. After the prayer meeting was over, I asked her what that meant, and she said God did not give her any revelation of that, she gave me what God told her to prophesy to me. I thought about that bridge for several days and went to my pastor for a revelation. He told me the same thing the prophetess had told me, "That God will give me the revelation." I went on with life's daily affairs and finally the Lord spoke to me in 2024, six years later after the prophecy was presented to me. He told me that this year the bridge He was carrying me across, conveys multifaceted meanings, complete healing of my health, not falling in the midst of my tests, trials, and tribulations. God was giving me strength to endure, not feeling the trauma that satan had planned for me in crossing over the bridge. God also gave me strength to withstand and tolerate any opposition as He carried me across the bridge. God was working on me, showing me how He sees me and in my heart there were some things that I needed to change and correct. He also told me a few months ago that He has finally carried me across the bridge, and I had made it to the end of the bridge. When He presented to me the things, I totally surrendered immediately and asked God to forgive me of the things He was not pleased with.

I am at the end of that bridge now and the hardest and most difficult parts are behind me. Satan knows this and is trying with breakneck speed to distract me with many of his tactics. I recognize him head on, which is why I can set my watch, knowing that my delivery date, my set time, and my appointed time are very near. They are within close range, I am right at the doorstep, especially in the vicinity.

Satan knows that he is throwing out all kinds of roadblocks, but I am "Walking It Out" until my appointed time by God has given me the CLEARANCE, to walk completely from the bridge on my own. I am looking and I am watching. I am FREE to move on to the next chapter in my life. Aretha Lae Coleman-Terry, You Are Free, You Are Free, Thank God Almighty, You Are Free, To Move On.

ABOUT THE AUTHOR

Dr. Aretha Coleman-Terry, a native of Memphis, Tennessee, is an ordained Elder known for her unwavering dedication to her church and community. With an impressive 35-year career at Legacy Shelby County Schools, Dr. Coleman-Terry has impacted countless lives through her commitment to education and mentoring. Her life is a testament to the power of faith, resilience, and compassion. Her tireless work within her church and community reflects her deep-rooted belief in the importance of giving back and supporting those in need. She generously shares the blessings she has received, using her experiences and resources to uplift and empower others.

Beyond her professional and philanthropic endeavors, Dr. Coleman-Terry is a devoted member of her faith community. She finds joy in spending time with her loved ones and draws strength from her church family and friends.

Dr. Coleman-Terry's life work is a shining example of how faith and dedication can create meaningful change in the world. Her legacy of service, both in her professional career and her philanthropic efforts, continues to inspire and uplift those around her. Through her heartfelt words and actions, Dr. Coleman-Terry aims to guide others toward a deeper understanding of faith, resilience, and the beauty of God's timing.

ALSO FROM
Dr. Aretha Coleman-Terry

My Roller Coaster Life Led Me to the Rock

A Spiritual Autobiography

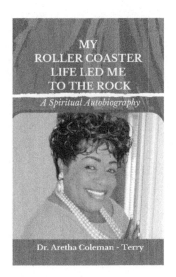

In this inspiring book, Dr. Coleman-Terry shares personal trials that led to an unwavering faith in Jesus, "the Rock." Growing up in a Christian home, the author learned the significance of prayer, faith, and favor, understanding that Jesus is the steadfast Rock to rely on during life's challenges. The book emphasizes the importance of daily fellowship with Jesus through prayer, fasting, and reading the Bible, promising peace and guidance. Aimed at youth facing various challenges, men navigating life's pressures, women building self-esteem, and unbelievers seeking enrichment, the author encourages all readers to find strength, peace, and purpose in their faith through the Rock.

Available on Amazon and other online booksellers.

Made in the USA
Monee, IL
17 August 2024

63445928R00089